Hope:

In A Lost And Fallen World

By: Only A. Guy

Hope In A Lost And Fallen World

Published by VIP Ink Publishing

Cover Art By Whyte Lady Designs L.L.C.
And
Sarah McClain   www.celemoe.com

www.onlyaguy.com
www.facebook.com/onlyaguy
www.twitter.com/onlyaguy1

www.vipinkpublishing.com

ISBN 13: 978-0-9847382-5-0
ISBN:0-9847382-5-0

Printed in the USA.

If you like this book here are some others coming out by this author you may find enjoyable as well as educational:

2011
Hard Questions About God
Hard Questions About Jesus
The Book Of Prayers

2012
Hard Questions About The Holy Spirit
Hard Questions About Heaven And Hell
Hard Questions About Angels And Demons
Hard Questions About Salvation
Hope In A Lost And Fallen World

2013
Hard Questions About The End Times
Hard Questions About Christianity
Hard Questions About Creation
Hard Questions About Humanity

2014
Hard Questions About Life's Decisions
Hard Questions About Cults And Religions
Hard Questions About False Doctrine
Hard Questions About Prayer
Hard Questions About Sin

Introduction

Billions today live with no hope. Yet all wish for better lives, a better to-morrow for themselves and their families. Most also recognize that the collective future of all nations seems equally hopeless. If one considers history, the course of the past 6,000 years, it is difficult to avoid pessi-mism. When the full picture is brought into view, when all facts are con-sidered, *this* world *is* hopeless. Modern civilization is beset, over-whelmed, with every conceivable problem, evil and ill that competitive, grasping, self-promoting human beings could devise. Having always been sick, it is now deep in terminal illness, wheezing out its final des-perate gasps before breathing its last.

The present world is a condemned building. It is like an old, empty row house, abandoned, overgrown, burned out, littered with trash, marred by broken windows and covered in graffiti. Built on a *poor foundation* from the beginning, its already weak underpinnings have now eroded to the point of collapse under its own weight. Like all condemned structures, dangerous if left standing, this "building" *must* come down. With "explosive charges" in place, it is soon to be imploded and the rubble scraped away in advance of a new and magnificent "world architecture" foretold long ago to replace it.

The plight of all nations today stands in stark contrast to the world that is coming, an artistic masterpiece soon to be unveiled. A fantastic future, truly incredible, lies ahead for every nation of the world! But it will not, and could never, occur under the hand of men.

Everything on earth begins with government. The governments of men do not, and have never, worked. They are themselves one of the biggest problems. These ineffective human inventions are unable to, and in fact will not "snatch victory from the jaws of defeat" at the last moment be-fore disaster!

But a better, perfect government, one not left to the devices, machina-tions and confusion of men, is coming. It will usher in peace, happiness, unity, abundance and prosperity for every human being and every coun-try on earth. While such a vision may seem impossible, it *will* happen—and in your lifetime!

It was always the Creator's Plan that a whole new and infinitely better world would come. One built from the beginning on a *good* foundation. A full third of the Bible is prophecy, history recorded in advance. Large sections of this describe the establishment of another world, one completely different from anything ever before seen on planet earth. The coming utopian age that God planned long ago will be absolutely marvelous, breathtaking to behold. It appears scripturally in vivid colors, with sharp outlines and exquisite detail, as a stunning, beautiful, panoramic and previously unimagined future world scope.

A wonderful new world *is* on the way, and this book offers an *advance preview*, an inside view!

Chapter I: Today's World

Most of what is occurring in today's world can only be described as ALL WRONG! Why, when things go wrong, do so few search for the cause?

Every effect, good or bad, can be traced to a root cause. Conversely, every cause brings an effect. Since the world is *filled* with bad effects, why do so few examine the cause? Why do scientists, educators, religionists and other "experts" and "thinkers" primarily devote their efforts to addressing these effects? Think for a moment. The world is filled with problems of every conceivable nature, and they are only growing worse, and greater in number. Therefore, the headlines of today's newspapers are filled with bad news. Here is a sampling of headlines we are all too familiar with:

- "War Rages in Middle East,"
- "Suicide Bombings Increase,"
- "Arms Race Reveals More Countries With Nukes,"
- "Man Kills Family, Then Self,"
- "Sniper Kills Ten, Wounds Twenty,"
- "HIV to Kill Ten Million Annually—and Rise,"
- "Ferry Overturns - One Thousand Lost,"
- "Mysterious Illness Kills Ten,"
- "Market Crashes - Global Recession, Even Depression, on Horizon,"
- "CEO Indicted - Two Billion Unaccounted For,"
- "God Banned From Schools,"
- "Teachers Losing Control of Classrooms,"
- "Typhoon Kills Thousands,"
- "Record Drought Grips North America - 500-year Flood in Europe,"
- "Pollution Chokes All Nations,"
- "More Huge Dead Zones Discovered in Oceans and Lakes,"
- "200,000 Starve to Death Daily,"
- "500 Million Contract Malaria Annually - 2.5 Million Children Die,"
- "5 of 6 Marriages Suffer Adultery,"
- "Two-thirds of Inner-City Births Illegitimate,"
- "3,000 Pornography Websites Appear Daily,"
- "Drug Lords Cause Civil War,"
- "Government Corruption Adds to Growing Cynicism & Voter Apathy,"
- "Riots Kill 75,"
- "Same-Sex Marriage Now Lawful!"

In reality, these headlines are reporting nothing more than a long list of bad effects. Since man does not know the causes, world problems only grow greater and humanity's general state of misery only seems to compound with the passing of time. Headlines scream worse and worse messages to those who can bear to read them. I ask, why?

But What If...?

While newspapers know that bad news sells, all long for good news in their own lives, and hope the world improves. Most people assume that, somehow, problems will eventually "work out alright," merely because they *want* them to. People *want* to enjoy peace, happiness, abundance, well-being, good health and general prosperity.

Could these things happen for everyone? Could they become universal? Could *all* the peoples of the world come to enjoy *all* these conditions? Is it possible that the problems now plaguing civilization on such a grand scale could abate...and eventually disappear? Could newspapers one day find themselves only able to report good news, everywhere? Instead of the above headlines, could these replace them:

- "Food Production Sufficient to Feed Entire World - With Plenty to Spare!"
- "All Chemical Fertilizers Banned - Soil Begins to Heal from Years of Neglect and Abuse!"
- "Food Now Much More Nutritious - and Tastes Better, Too!"
- "All Deadly Viruses Eradicated - Including HIV, Ebola, West Nile, Polio and Smallpox!"
- "All Lethal Bacteria Disappear - Including E. coli, Tuberculosis, Cholera, Staphylococcus, Salmonella and Bubonic Plague!"
- "No More Fatal Illness - Cancer, Strokes, Heart Disease, Diabetes and Other Killers Now Gone!"
- "All Blind, Deaf and Crippled Made Whole in Mass Worldwide Healing!"
- "No More Sickness - Millions Report Perfect Health!"
- "All Hospitals and Clinics Put Out of Business - Millions of Doctors, Nurses, Staff and Paramedics Find More Useful Vocations!"
- "All Pharmaceutical Companies Re-oriented and Re-educated to Wise Use of Herbs and Vitamins!"
- "Health 'Breaks Out' Everywhere - All Report 'No Problems'!"
- "Divorce Disappears - No More Broken Families!"
- "No More Fraudulent Marriages - Prenuptial Agreements No Longer Necessary!"
- "All Teenagers Practice Respect and Obedience to Parents and Authority!"
- "All Deadbeat Dads Take Responsibility and Find Employment!"

- "All Mothers Find Nurturing Children at Home Rewarding!"
- "War Outlawed Around the World - All Nations Disarmed!"
- "Destructive Weapons Destroyed and Recycled!"
- "All Military Personnel Moving into Construction Projects - Rebuilding Bridges and Critical Infrastructure!"
- "Many Lands Recover From Civil War - Being Resettled and Farmed Productively!"
- "Global Trade Competition Ceases - Nations Cooperate Fully!"
- "No More Crime - All Rates Plunge to Zero!"
- "Murder - Thing of the Past!"
- "Armed Robbery Disappears - So Does Fear!"
- "All Thieves Repent - Now Seeking Honest Employment!"
- "City Streets Now Safe - Children Play Freely in Once Dangerous Neighborhoods!"
- "Education Now Focuses on Right Values - No More 'Situation Ethics,' Secular Humanism and 'No Absolutes'!"
- "Bible Taught in All Schools!"
- "All Peoples Speak and Learn One Language!"
- "Law of 'Cause and Effect' Revealed - Explains Why Past Disease, War, Famine, Poverty, Ignorance and Misery!"
- "Weather Revolution Brings Stability to World!"
- "Today's Weather - Beautiful Skies and Rain in Due Season Tomorrow!" –
- "Deserts Blossom Worldwide - Now Favorite Garden Spots!"
- "Earthquakes, Volcanoes, Hurricanes and Floods No Longer a Threat!"

Do these headlines sound impossible? They are not; actually, they are a *certainty*. A wonderful, prophesied utopian world is coming to planet earth. It *will* happen soon, in *your* lifetime! But that time is not yet.

The Hope of Many

Many scientists and experts believe the world is evolving toward a higher, and better, order. They see the future as a wonderful time of exciting, unending possibilities. They see general betterment of the human condition, medical advancement, improvement in agriculture, producing more & better food, and scientific breakthroughs undreamed of now. These thinkers are so hopeful that they barely recognize the severity and complexity of the world's problems.

They live in a dream world, and wear rose-tinted glasses that filter out the harsh reality of the world around us. But they do represent one popular school of thought. Only when the brutal reality of world-shattering conditions and events slams into them will they realize their hopes were only a pipedream. They will learn that God will work things out in a way that they were not prepared for. But He will not use the "magic" of science to pull a rabbit out of the hat, as so many hope and suppose. This is not how God will save men from themselves at the last possible moment before they blast themselves from the planet!

A Coming Super Government?

Numerous scientists recognize that the planet and civilization *are* on a collision course with calamity! Many are scared, and their statements of what could happen are frightening. They speak of the need for one world *super government* to stop mankind's runaway problems. Yet virtually no one believes such a government would work if it were in the hands of men. The obstacles just to achieve the government, to say nothing of *how* it would solve man's exploding troubles and ills, are enormous. But there is good news!

The Bible is almost entirely a message about a coming world government. Everywhere Christ went, He preached, *announced*, the coming of the kingdom of God. He explained that it would be a world-ruling government that would smash and replace all the governments of men. He brought exciting, thrilling good news, in *advance* of its arrival. He spoke of a utopian, wonderful world tomorrow, now *imminent*, explaining how many would qualify to rule with Him. But the world of His day was not ready to receive His message.

When Christ comes He will possess vast power to affect change of every kind. He will be crowned as King of kings, *other* kings will rule with Him and the nations of the world will at first resist Him. But, He will *force* them to be happy, healthy and prosperous, enjoying the abundant life. How ironic that mankind will have to be required, FORCED, to accept and enjoy these conditions.

Later, we will examine that world in detail, including all who will be a part of it. We will learn how it will be governed. We will also understand *how* all the world's troubles, evils and problems will vanish, *why* there will be no more of the insoluble problems which today bring misery for most of humanity. But mankind will not produce or bring these things. All this will be done *to*, not *by*, men!

The Harsh Reality of Today's World

Before we can examine the exciting, thrilling and wonderful world of tomorrow, we need to take a look at the harsh reality of the world today. It is not a pretty picture.

Modern technology has resulted in breathtaking scientific, medical, and industrial advancements

Meanwhile; war, poverty, famine, disease and destruction have never been worse.

The world is *filled* with problems and troubles of every sort:

- disease,
- pollution,
- poverty,
- ignorance,
- religious confusion,
- war,
- terrorism,
- crime,
- violence,
- hunger,
- immorality,
- slavery,
- oppression,
- political upheaval and much more.

The passing of time brings *more* problems, not less. Also, existing problems grow collectively worse instead of better. Why, at every turn, has mankind bungled and botched all efforts to solve his truly great problems? We need to take a long, thorough look at what is wrong with this world, and why the crescendo of problems engulfing it are far beyond mankind's ability to even successfully define and address, let alone solve.

People have never seemed less able to address and overcome their own personal problems. As with the world in general, individuals and families are drowning under an ever-greater sea of moral decadence and seemingly insurmountable difficulties. More and more people seem completely incapable of managing their lives.

Men have created many amazing technological inventions, but they cannot create *solutions to worldwide problems*. Mankind has harnessed the capability of computers to process vast amounts of information, but human beings cannot *correctly process personal problems*. Scientists have discovered much about the size, magnificence and precision of the universe, but they cannot *discover the way to peace*. Astronomers can find majestic, beautiful new galaxies throughout the universe, but they cannot find a way to *preserve the beauty and majesty of earth*. Scientists have also unleashed the power of the atom, but are powerless to *unleash answers to life's greatest questions*. Educators have taught millions how to earn a living, but not *how to live!*

The well-known presidential historian and columnist Peggy Noonan summarized the complex, jumbled course that has been mankind's history: "In the long ribbon of history, life has been one long stained and tangled mess, full of famine, horror, war and disease. We must have thought we had it better because man had improved. But man doesn't really 'improve,' does he? Man is man. Human nature is human nature; the impulse to destroy coexists with the desire to build and create and make better" ("America's Age of Uncertainty," *Akron Beacon Journal*, Nov. 9, 2001).

Men's Governments Do Not Work

Again we ask:

- *Why* is the world filled with problems, evils and ills of every sort?
- *Why* is it in such a state of confusion and ignorance?
- *How* did it come to be this way?
- *Why* do men's governments never permanently solve problems, only postpone ill effects, while at the same time creating new problems?

You may have supposed that the governments of modern nations reflect God's way. This is almost everyone's assumption. While God does, in fact, establish and remove nations, this is not His world. This is why Christ foretold the arrival of a great super government to replace the confused, ineffective, inefficient governments of men, so powerless to solve any of the world's biggest problems.

Why cannot the governments of men get along, avoid war, and find peace and agreement? *Why* is there constant instability, scandal and division among leaders, and seemingly endless revolutions and military coups?

Why is there no shortage of demagogues, dictators and revolutionaries, always promising to make things better, yet only able to preside over a continual worsening of problems and conditions?

Look at the governments of this world. Generally speaking, there are three types today; *monarchies, dictatorships* and *democracies.*

Monarchies involve nobility, royalty, where bloodline is the key to succession of power. Through the death of a king or queen, a succeeding prince or princess ascends the throne. This can last for a few generations or many centuries. Generally, monarchies are eventually replaced, either violently or peacefully, with the king or queen permitted to retain minimal power.

Dictatorships and totalitarian governments are usually created through violence, by coup or revolution. They are often short-lived because something similar, or a democracy, quickly replaces them.

Democracies and Republics are best described as collaborative, representative or parliamentarian. Officials and leaders are elected, representing "the will of the people", this involves a voting or balloting process in the selection of one candidate in preference to one or several others. This form is generally considered to be the best of mankind's governments. Yet, the great 20th-century British Prime Minister, Winston Churchill, called democracy "the *worst* form of government - *except for all the others.*" This shows an amazing insight into how democracy really works, from an insider's view.

But as bad as democracy may be, it is far better than any *other* form of government in the hands of men. Democracy at least attempts to insure more individual "freedoms" than other kinds of humanly-devised government.

In the end, however, none of man's governments work very well nor for very long. If the "best" of man's forms of government is always ultimately ineffective in resolving a country's largest problems, then where lies the answer to the great problems of civilization? How will they be permanently resolved so that the utopian world that writers, philosophers, politicians, and the masses, long for can become reality?

If crime is to stop, if poverty is to vanish, if war is to be gone, if disease is to be wiped out, if famine is to be eradicated, if pollution is to cease, if ignorance is to disappear, if religious confusion is to be removed, there must be a REASON. The cause or causes of these things must be identified, and removed, before all the good effects prophesied for tomorrow can replace the widespread bad effects of today.

Food, Water, Pollution and Population

Consider some of the terrible conditions on earth today, which are predicted to grow far worse by the year 2050, should events remain unchecked. Many of the following statistics come from the United Nation's "The State of World Population 2001" report. It is a thorough report that makes for a sobering read.

Throughout history, men have been oppressed by corrupt, power-hungry dictators.

The world population has more than tripled in the last seventy years, to 6.1 billion. It has doubled since 1960, and is predicted to reach between 9.3 and 10.9 billion by 2050. The forty-nine poorest, least-developed nations will actually triple to a population of nearly two billion. This worldwide population growth will bring staggering problems!

Just 2.5 percent of the earth's water is fresh. Only 20 percent of this (or 0.5 percent) is accessible ground or surface water. Current population needs consume 54 percent of this available water. By 2050 it will be 90 percent, because the earth grows by 77 million additional people per year requiring an amount of water equivalent to the mighty Rhine River every year. Also, developing countries dump, untreated, 90-95 percent of sewage and 70 percent of industrial waste into surface waters. Population growth guarantees that this problem will only grow worse. In addition, chemical runoff from fertilizers, pesticides and acid rain sufficiently ruin water quality, making it unusable. Some experts predict the world will also completely run out of usable drinking water by 2050. *Take a moment to consider just this single staggering thought!*

Population growth continues to outpace food production. There are 800 million people who are chronically malnourished and 2 billion who lack "food security." Only fifteen crop species provide 90 percent of the world's food, yet it is estimated that 60,000 different plant species could reach extinction by just 2025! Yet, by that year, the projected 8 billion inhabitants of earth will require twice today's food needs, with greatly improved distribution, to eradicate hunger. But few experts see this as remotely possible.

Today's world is full of overcrowded, smog filled cities. Pollution, drought and dwindling, contaminated water supplies are all leading to man's final hour. Each day, 160,000 people move from rural areas to cities. This is happening fastest in under-developed countries. Enormous problems are resulting from sanitation, overcrowding, access to modern health services and the ability of schools to absorb the increase of students. Fully 60% of all disease on earth is sanitation-related. Air pollution kills nearly 3 million people in developing countries alone every year, with poor sanitation killing another 12 million each year! Various forms of indoor air pollution affect 2.5 *billion* people a year and kill 2.2 million. Changes in climate are also altering the zones of risk for insect-borne diseases. New and more virulent diseases are appearing or reappearing. Many bacteria are proving to be drug-resistant because of the ongoing over-prescribing of antibiotics.

Some problems predicted for the future? Limited and diminishing arable land, deforestation, urbanization, shrinking size of family farms, degradation of the land, shortages and degradation of water, irrigation problems, waste buildup, greenhouse gases and changes of climate, greater intensity and frequency of severe weather, causing flooding and loss of crops, and the permanent loss of certain types of crops. Together, they spell untold calamity, and even catastrophe, for a mankind unprepared to solve these and many other problems.

While the world is suffering from "information overload," none of that overload is truly addressing the number and complexity of mankind's growing list of *insoluble* problems. Even with all of his creative ingenuity and intelligence, man cannot solve the most important problems that threaten his very existence on an earth that he is systematically destroying.

The Limits to Growth

There have been studies seeking to determine how fast, how far, and how big the population of humanity can grow before it, or the earth, can no longer support it.

Thomas R. Malthus, an early nineteenth century economist, considered three factors as the primary "correction factors" of population—*war*, *famine* and *disease*. Malthus predicted eventual disaster because the world population would eventually outrun the food supply. Many of his modern disciples maintain that this rendezvous with disaster has intensified, due to the increased population growth rate. Much of this acceleration is due to the use of vaccinations and antibiotics, which have reduced the effect of diseases, thus "exacerbating" the population bomb.

The "Malthusian Specter," as this dilemma is known, is an ever-increasing grim reality. Two publications; "The Limits to Growth," Potomac Associates, 1972 and "Mankind at the Turning Point," Dutton, 1974; spelled out a number of computer models that extended existing trends throughout the 21st century. The models were based on five variables:

- Population,
- food production,
- industrialization,
- pollution and
- consumption of non-renewable natural resources.

Even without the complications and effects of a major war or disastrous weather patterns, these models consistently projected a virtual collapse of civilization by the middle of the 21st century, around the year 2050!

Among the critics of these findings were such wild optimists as Dr. Herman Kahn of the Hudson Institute of New York. Kahn predicted an incredible utopia for the near future in which the industrialized world would enjoy more leisure than ever before. He did acknowledge that idleness would spawn more social unrest and possibly more drug use. Though he had confidence that *infrastructure* problems, such as pollution, disease and water supply, will be reduced by technology, he had no answers for enormous *social* dilemmas.

Concerning food production for the exploding population, Kahn, in his book, *The Next 200 Years*, stated, "Food will be extracted from almost any organic matter, including wood, leaves, cellulose, petroleum, and even agricultural waste." He was even confident that technology would insure that starvation could be averted. But consider the price to be paid in food *quality*, if what he said would even be possible. Kahn added, "There will be no scarcity of food in the next 200 years. If output from conventional farming isn't sufficient, let 'em eat waste." **Incredible!** One can only wonder what type of existence such "optimists" have in store for the quality of life in *their* utopia.

While strongly criticizing Malthus' students and their computer models, the optimists labeled them as "doomsayers." However, as Kahn's predictions demonstrate, such optimists are removed from reality, and even rational thought. Yet the world has generally ignored warnings to the contrary. Keep in mind that the "doomsayers" simply provided information for computers to process, also hoping for a favorable result. The optimists ignore these warnings and accuse the computers' programs as being "pessimistic." Although the conditions remain more threatening than ever, it is just not *politically correct* to express, or even suggest, pessimism.

No matter what human beings choose to believe, the time bomb, threatening all human life, continues to tick. The delicate balance of numerous dangerous factors is so fragile that just a major war could spell doom for man's survival. In *Matthew 24:22*, Christ warned of the grave threat of war to human existence mostly by weapons of mass destruction. But there is a much broader dimension to the threat to human existence than just surviving a catastrophic war. After 6,000 years of man going his own way, humanity has approached the brink of extinction on several fronts. Overpopulation coupled with worldwide pollution, famine and resulting disease epidemics, carries the potential to wipe out all of humanity, and leave earth a dead planet!

Next, we consider the most dangerous catalyst given us by science and technology - warfare. This is widely used by the nations of today's world and characterizes how men seek results through the use of devastating destruction.

The Constant of War

The horror of war has wracked the world for thousands of years. Its fruits are terror, destruction, economic upheaval, orphaned children, population displacement, widespread devastation of the land, atrocities, hunger, disease, untold suffering, misery, despair, injuries, death and even genocide. All these yield even greater hatred and revenge, endless retaliation, and more war, because nothing is ever permanently resolved through military conflict.

Yet, no one has ever been able to properly address and remove the specter of war. Ever since Cain killed Abel *Genesis 4*, human history has been a chronicle of war. What began as family or tribal disagreements later developed into conflicts between nations. The one-sided conflict between Cain and Abel was motivated by jealousy and contempt. And so have been the agendas of virtually all nations throughout history.

Also, long-standing ethnic, tribal and religious differences, coupled with boundary disputes and outright aggression to seize the land or property of others, always served to fuel the next war fought between the same peoples or nations. This means that war has at least indirectly affected *all* nations in *every* period of history. Many countries have made war their primary means of livelihood, not just a means of defense or protection. Those nations that chose not to actively pursue military conflict had to at least expend time, money and effort to protect themselves. Sometimes having to "buy" peace, by paying tribute to powers that could have dominated them.

In the mid-1960s, a Norwegian statistician programmed a computer to count all of the wars through the 6,000 years of mankind's history. The conclusion was that 14,531 wars had been fought. This was merely the number of known and recorded wars. How many more were not? And consider that this was several decades ago. Countless hundreds more, either between or within nations, have been fought since then. Of course, this does not count the endless stream of terrorist acts, such as suicide/homicide bombings, commando raids and other assaults, and now serial snipers, which occur in "undeclared" wars.

The incredible new weapons that technology has given us, forever altered the face of war. "Smart" bombs, which are laser-guided to bring precision and efficiency to the art of killing, have replaced many types of "dumb" bombs. Military scientists have also developed cluster bombs, called "daisy cutters" because they cut down large numbers of human beings like a lawnmower cuts grass. Also, there are new bombs called "bunker busters" that can penetrate deep into the earth in pursuit of enemies hiding in caves, before detonating and killing the inhabitants. More and better precision-guided missiles are also continually appearing.

Various highly lethal attack aircraft now exist; helicopters, jets, bombers, gunships; that have brought conventional warfare to a pinnacle of destructive capability never before known. A 2,000-pound, precision, satellite-guided bomb has a "kill zone" of 1,300 yards radius (almost three quarters of a mile). It kills and maims indiscriminately. So this can some-

14

times involve "friendly fire" casualties, in which one's own troops are hit. This is generally considered to be "acceptable and necessary collateral damage."

Modern military thinkers and strategists are now forced to think and talk in terms of protection from, or utilization of, "weapons of mass destruction." The killing capability of nuclear, chemical and biological weapons and now radiological, or "dirty bombs," are almost indescribably horrible. Yet these weapons are now apparently in the hands of unstable countries and regimes, which may not be fully capable of controlling their use or safeguarding their inventory.

This is why the famous American General, Douglas MacArthur, declared, "Men since the beginning of time have sought peace...Military alliances, balances of power, leagues of nations, all in turn failed, leaving the only path to be by way of the crucible of war. The utter destructiveness of war now blocks out this alternative. We have had our last chance. If we will not devise some greater and more equitable system, our Armageddon will be at our door. The problem basically is theological and involves a *spiritual* recrudescence, an improvement of human *character* that will synchronize with our almost matchless advances in science, art, literature, and all material and cultural developments of the past two thousand years. It must be of the spirit if we are to save the flesh" (April 19, 1951, speech to Congress).

Man's creative abilities, coupled with world tension, lust and greed, have led to the amassing of a sophisticated arsenal of super weapons. Bear in mind that this speech was given over fifty years ago! Since that time, wars have continued to flourish. Men and nations have sought to justify this state of affairs through rationalizing and moralizing about the "inevitability" and "necessity" of going to war. While political hawks and doves argue endlessly about war and peace; and demonstrations, protests and debates mount; none consider that mankind does not know the *way* to peace (*Isaiah 59:8; Romans 3:17*). Yet religious leaders ignore God's Word and debate the definition of a "just war", and listening becomes a study in confusion, blindness and deceit. There is no such thing as a "just war." All war is horrible. But these never ending debates do reflect mankind's belief that he can "fix the world" through various programs that never work in the end. As a result, humanity has entered the final countdown to World War III!

Famine in the Developed World

No discussion of war is complete without examining the conditions that inevitably follow in its wake. The biggest is famine, and it now stalks much of the world. Famines are not generally classified as a sudden disaster, but rather a drawn-out process. While slow-moving drought is; and has always been; the most *common* cause the aftermath of war is the single *biggest* cause of wide scale famine.

Silently, ominously, the specter of famine has spread in the past century. So far, this has primarily occurred in second and third world countries. Technology and man's best innovative efforts have not stemmed the tide. More than ever, famine looms over every nation because men and governments ignore the causes.

So far-reaching are the effects of modern civilization on the environment that industrial, residential and transportation pollution have begun to affect earth's weather patterns, and thus increase the prospect of famine. Persistent droughts, in critical areas of underdeveloped and overpopulated nations, bring horrible famines. The fragile ecosystem of a struggling earth is threatened by these trends.

Consider the demographic distribution of the U.S. population, past and present. Ninety-five percent of the original American colonists lived on farms. Today, only two percent of the U.S. population are farmers and ranchers. Facts suggest that the two percent will continue to shrink.

Recognize this; the large supermarket retailers only carry a three-to-four-day inventory on their shelves. During blizzards and ice storms, people invariably empty the shelves in one day. Imagine what will happen when terrible upheaval or panic strikes in the wake of future wide-scale disasters.

Starvation affects human beings in a profoundly different way than do other catastrophes. The deprivation of needed nutrients lowers the natural immunity and increases susceptibility to diseases. Psychological effects include fear, uncertainty and dependency, which can escalate on both individual and collective levels. When people are faced with the impending threat of starvation, they almost always become *aggressive*. Casualties tend to be losers of a furious battle for survival, rather than passive victims who simply gave in.

The Threat of Diseases and Epidemics

Science once believed that it could control and conquer disease. But, again, new diseases are emerging and older ones, like tuberculosis, are rapidly mutating into antibiotic-resistant forms. The medical world is quickly losing its main weapon in the war against disease. Hardly a week passes without reports of new disease outbreaks somewhere in the world. The danger is greatest in underdeveloped nations, where poor sanitation, war, overcrowding, and poverty spawn epidemics.

Cholera, dysentery, typhoid and malaria are still rampant. Add to this the more recent arrivals of such threats as the Ebola virus, Hantavirus, E. coli bacteria, Salmonella virus, West Nile virus, and Mad Cow disease. Then add to this list the dangerous bacteria spread by biological warfare and terrorism. While the strains causing the most concern are Anthrax and Smallpox, these are far from the only possible disease epidemics on the horizon.

Also, many cultures treat disease through the eyes of entrenched, pervasive superstition. Consider South Africa, where the HIV virus is a rampant epidemic. Witch doctors tell people that having sex with a virgin is the only way to purge the virus from one's system. Millions believe them and many attempt to carry it out. Babies have become the safest and surest choice for such "purging." In just one case, ten adults used a single baby. This is but a tiny snapshot of what superstition causes today.

Just the threat of devastating epidemics is now probably more than civilization can bear. The world's resources have become stretched to the limit. At the end of 6,000 years of man's rule, in which Satan is the real unseen ruler, civilization is nearing complete breakdown and set to take the Earth with it. Social values are rapidly unraveling and the population bomb is ticking. All while optimists discuss an imaginary utopia!

Breakdown of the Family

Next we examine the basic building block of any society, *the family*. In our search for some statistic to provide hope for civilization, we must examine the social fabric. How stable are modern families? Solid family structure reliably predicts social stability. However, the absence of a solid family structure is a revealing indicator of impending social upheaval and instability. The collection of statistics, facts and trends listed below reveals the pattern, with all too painful clarity. While shocking, this is only a thumbnail of available information:

- 50 percent of married women and 66 percent of married men in the U.S. commit adultery (combined, these statistics indicate that over 80 percent of marriages involve at least one adulterous partner).
- Only 25 percent of Brazilians expect their spouses to remain faithful.
- Same-sex marriage is now legal in a growing number of countries.
- Compared to first marriages, remarriages are 50 percent more likely to end in divorce during the first five years, tend to be unstable, break up more often, and more quickly (*Statistics Canada*, Canadian Census Bureau).
- One of the most authoritative studies ever done in the U.S. on mental health found that the divorced are nearly twice as likely to suffer from a mental illness as those who are married. They are 6 to 10 times more likely to use inpatient psychiatric facilities and 4 to 5 times more likely to be clients in outpatient clinics.
- Divorced status is the fastest growing marital category. The number of divorcees has more than quadrupled from 4.3 million in 1970 to 18.3 million in 1996.
- Divorces per 1,000 marriages:
    - ⇒ 1969 - 40;
    - ⇒ 1990 - 380 (up 171 percent);
    - ⇒ 1996 - 451 (up 221 percent since 1969).

The divorce-to-marriage ratio in the U.S. has approached the 50 percent range for the past decade. Though divorces have slightly declined in the same proportion as marriages have declined, this is only because of the huge increase in live-in relationships, which circumvent both marriage and divorce. Recent decades have seen an alarming increase in single-parent families, resulting in numerous additional social problems.

The Role of Media

Most experts agree that modern exposure to media is perhaps the most detrimental influence. In much of the Western world, endless television programs belittle marriage, while openly *promoting* gay and lesbian rela-tionships. Fornication and adultery are routinely portrayed, and *endorsed*, in virtually every heterosexual relationship. To think otherwise is to be considered woefully politically incorrect and unprogressive. Take a mo-ment. Think about today's movies and television programs. How long has it been since a series either promoted, or even endorsed, the concept of the wholesome families so common in the 50s and 60s?

Stigmas against divorce and "shacking up" have basically vanished. So has the idea that marriage is a lifelong commitment. Most young adults have no real understanding of why past generations so strongly defended the family or why they held contempt for those who openly lived together unmarried. The fear of violating, once deeply ingrained, biblically -based, moral beliefs has almost disappeared in today's world. Most modern psychologists and leaders, caught in the tailspin of degenerate and generally promiscuous practices, are quick to defend them by falling back on the modern cliché: "Who are you to condemn me? This is my lifestyle!"

Dr. James Billinger, Professor of Social Science and Humanities at Princeton University, has succinctly addressed this trend; "Life [modern life] itself sometimes seems suddenly drained of substance, let alone moral standards, by the continued use of that dreadful word: 'lifestyle.' If life is just a matter of style, one style is just as good as another, and another is probably better, and the other one is maybe the best of all. But no one can live that way and no society will long endure or even cohere without some basic moral standard. Sooner or later, they will be imposed from without if they are not found within." Dr. Billinger's implied day of reckoning cannot be far away.

Worldwide Bombardment

Let's examine more directly how social trends, mixed with negative media influences, have affected the modern generation. Media influence dominates the lives of youth with messages from Hollywood, Madison Avenue and MTV, all *glamorizing* rebellious attitudes, immorality and self-centeredness. Consider the Internet, with a few clicks of a button, children can access web pages that promote every sick idea known to man. Photographs of twisted and perverted images are only seconds away.

Mass media has made this the age of instant gratification. Decadent television, awful degenerate music and music videos, sexually explicit movies, incredibly violent video games and trendy, style-conscious teen magazines all deceive children into believing that they are the center of the universe. Children of this age are constantly bombarded with messages of selfishness, greed and the "me first" attitude.

Here is a sampling of alarming statistics on a variety of subjects resulting from the media assault upon youth, coupled with the vulnerability of many coping with unstable home situations:
- 75% of children of divorce also end up going through a divorce.

- Children from divorced families drop out of school at twice the rate of children from intact families.
- Among teenage and adult females, parental divorce is linked to lower confidence, earlier sexual activity, greater delinquency, and difficulty establishing fulfilling, lasting adult heterosexual relationships. Yet the divorce usually occurred years before any difficulties were observed.
- The best indicator of potential teen suicide is parental divorce and living with only one parent.
- Most children watch a staggering 5,000-plus hours of television by the time they enter the first grade—and will have watched over 19,000 hours by the end of high school. This is more time than they will have spent in class!
- By age 18, a youth will have witnessed an astonishing 200,000 acts of violence on TV, including 40,000 murders.
- From 1992 to 1999, students were more likely to be victims of theft at school than anywhere else.
- From July 1, 1998 to June 30, 1999, there were 47 violent deaths in U.S. schools.
- The U.S. has the highest total of teen pregnancy of any industrialized nation; one million annually among girls ages 15-19.
- Per capita, the United Kingdom is first in teen pregnancy, with about half a million pregnancies. Recently, it was reported that a 16-year-old U.K. teen had been pregnant ten times since age 12. She has had two children, three abortions and five miscarriages!
- Another result of rampant immorality is that each year, about 25 percent of new HIV cases occur in people ages 13-21.
- Perhaps most horrible is that 19 million U.S. teens alone contracted a sexually-transmitted disease from 1997-2001. That's just five years! The untold suffering this represents, coupled with such rampant, epidemic immorality, could only be described as a social *holocaust*!

Current social and immoral trends show no sign of reversal, but rather a worsening, with media leading the way. The emerging picture is one of a civilization *completely incapable* of providing nations and peoples with enough social stability to survive. Any voice of reason is as "one crying in the wilderness" against howling gale force winds. Such are denigrated as "virtuecrats" or "morality police" hung up on old values and morals.

Exploding Drug and Alcohol Abuse

Another fallout from the deterioration of values is the specter of drug abuse. Worldwide, the *United Nations World Drug Report 2000* estimated that as many as 180 million people are drug users. Substance abuse is truly a global phenomenon, with affluent nations the worst.

Despite the fact that the U.S. government spent $1.65 billion in 1982 on the war against drugs, and this amount increased annually to $17.7 billion by 1999, the problem is still growing. In 2000, an estimated 14 million Americans were illicit drug users. This staggering number is strictly based on arrests, surveys and a few other contributing factors. The actual number of drug abusers is projected to be *much higher*. In fact, during this period, *half* of all students admitted trying an illegal drug before graduating from high school. How many did not admit it?

In addition to the mounting dilemma of drugs, the problems of alcohol are much more costly. In 1992, the U.S. spent $166 billion to combat the alcohol problem, roughly $800 paid by each adult. The amount in 1995 rose an estimated 12.5 percent to over $200 billion. Alcohol is involved in three out of ten automobile accidents, and is involved in nearly *half* of all violent crime. As dramatic as these statistics sound, the worst part is that they are steadily climbing with no end in sight.

Exploding Crime

Society is being plagued by an ever-increasing crime problem. Not only is it a continual topic among news headlines, but the severity and inhumanity of criminal acts are also worsening. U.S. statistics alone show that every half hour an astonishing 59 aggravated assaults and 90 violent crimes, including one murder, are committed. How long can such conditions exist, and they are growing worse, before citizens are literally prisoners of fear in their own homes?

According to the World Health Organization, violence is responsible for the deaths of more than 1.6 million people worldwide every year. It is "among the leading causes of death for people aged 15-44 years of age, accounting for 14 percent of deaths among males and 7 percent of deaths among females. On an average day, 1,424 people are killed in acts of homicide, almost one person every minute" (*The World Report on Violence and Health*, Oct. 3, 2002).

Terrorism and the spreading epidemic of youth crime are two of the biggest issues amidst the world's growing social problems. New York City alone employs 72,000 police officers in an effort to combat its escalating crime rate. They are still losing the battle.

People seem to no longer consider the effects of their actions on others. They rationalize that their actions will have no adverse effects on others, or that they themselves are victims. Many openly justify crimes of terror through the belief that any suffering they inflict on others is ultimately for good and merely an acceptable means to an end.

While statistics do indicate a drop in the overall U.S. crime rate between 1991 and 2001 (note these were economic boom times), such figures dwarf statistics as recent as forty years ago. Recently, it was learned that murder rates would be *five times higher* if medical advances and emergency response had not improved dramatically. Now, all preliminary indications are that the actual murder rates are rising again. Also, it has been estimated that over 1,500 Russian gangs are operating in the U.S. alone! Current studies also show that over two-thirds of the world's countries are rife with corruption.

God's Word shows that conditions will grow worse, resulting in a worldwide explosion of lawlessness, just prior to Christ's Return. *Matthew 24:3, 12* describes a time of lawlessness ("iniquity") that parallels the time of Noah before the Flood *(vs. 37)*.

What were world conditions like at that time? Read this: *"The earth also was corrupt before God, and the earth was filled with violence. And God looked upon the earth, and, behold, it was corrupt; for all flesh had corrupted his way upon the earth. And God said unto Noah, The end of all flesh is come before Me; for the earth is filled with violence through them; and, behold, I will destroy them with the earth"* (Gen. 6:11-13).

The Magnet of Materialism

Meanwhile, the world stands aghast at the marvels of science and technology. Many religiously trust in them as the deliverer from all of mankind's problems and woes. Truly, many scientific and technological innovations have made many tasks far more efficient, while greatly increasing productivity. Many of these innovations have translated into more luxurious and efficient transportation, instant communication, greater convenience and more "toys" for use in leisure time.

But within the realm of technology, the shift toward materialism has been undeniable. Especially in the West, materialism has become an obsession for most. This obsession has led directly to the emergence of a modern mix of humanism (emphasis on one's interests and values) and hedonism, the belief that happiness and enjoyment of the "here and now" is the central purpose of life.

While anti-communist, the famous Russian author and philosopher, Aleksander Solzhenitsyn, made some profound observations on Western trends and materialism. Here is an excerpt from his commencement address given at Harvard University in June 1978: "People today constantly seek more and greater pleasures instead of God (*II Tim. 3:4*)... The Western world has now sunk to such a level of spiritual exhaustion, that I could not recommend your society in its present state as an ideal for the transformation of ours [former Soviet-led East]. In fact, the West has been so dulled by materialism and the constant desire to have still more things and an even better life that it is simply no match for the sterner societies of the Eastern world where life's complexity and mortal weight have produced stronger, deeper, and more interesting character than those generated by standardized Western well-being... If humanism were right in declaring that man is born to be happy, he would not be born to die. Since his body is doomed to die, his task on earth evidently must be of a more spiritual nature. It cannot be unrestrained enjoyment of everyday life. It cannot be the search for the best ways to obtain material goods and then cheerfully get the most out of them. It has to be the fulfillment of a permanent, earnest duty so that one's life journey may become an experience of moral growth, in that one may leave life a better human being than one started it... The human soul longs for things higher, warmer and purer than those offered by today's mass living habits, introduced by the revolting invasion of publicity, by television stupor and by intolerable music."

What amazing insight into the materialism gripping the West, and this was said over 25 years ago!

The direction of civilization is only partially influenced by governments, religion and education. In the modern Western world, it appears that media, movies and television, bear far more influence upon youth and the general population than the influence of government, religion and education combined!

When the foundational reasons for human existence revolve around materialism, any civilization has almost run its course. The West, and most of the rest of the world, has passed a point of no return. The signs are everywhere.

Education

If a tree is known by its fruit, look at the *fruits* of modern education. They are:

- cynicism
- skepticism
- rejection of values
- widespread immorality
- drunkenness and endless partying
- protests
- focus on diversity,
- political correctness,
- emphasis on being "cool" and accepted and,
- rebellion in general

All these are in place of acquiring the necessary important knowledge to succeed. Such a system is doomed!

The institutions of education spawn society's leaders. Most of the values that people hold were acquired during basic education. The *Encyclopedia Britannica 11th Edition* defines education as "an attempt on the part of adult members of a human society to shape the development of the coming generation in accordance with its *own ideals* of life" (Vol. 8, p. 951).

The true ideals of life have been passed over by societies cut off from God. Plato, the Greek philosopher who founded the academic system, expressed the direct aim of education in terms based upon false pagan ideas. The injection of pagan thought has been integral to education for many generations.

Also, for centuries, the great universal church has greatly influenced education with additional pagan traditions. The world has always been dominated by forces that oppose the truth and the knowledge of God. Educators have duped generations into believing the evolutionary lie. Evolution, essentially the explanation of a creation without a creator, is taught throughout all the industrialized nations. Men would rather reject special creation and evidence of intelligent design, preferring the nonsensical, unproven; actually *dis*proven; theory of evolution. Increasingly, school systems *require* evolution to be taught, while tacitly *permitting* "creationism" to be mentioned. This has caused generations to believe that mankind is continually evolving into a better and higher order of existence. Look around and you will see the fruits of the great deception. In fact, the whole world has been kept in darkness by these false teachings that contradict the truths of God. Mankind is not evolving upward, he is degenerating downward, into worse and worse decadence and immorality.

One of the best statements about the failed, bankrupt education of this world was written by Professor Emeritus Dr. Donald M. Dozer of the University of California at Santa Barbara. It is from his article "Educational Humbuggery": "Ours is an age dominated by half-truths, and for this situation many causes can be found, not the least of which are attributable to the processes of higher education…American universities have succumbed to the cult of faddism, sensationalism, and even vulgarism. New courses in scatology, whether masquerading as sociology, anthropology, or literature, have been given classroom platforms and respectability…As students have become increasingly involved in curricular planning they have encouraged the idea that courses rich in content inhibit their creative impulses and represent an imposition upon them. This has led to the multiplication of colleges of creative studies, which might better be called colleges of undisciplined studies where lectures are eschewed as 'bourgeois' and students educate themselves in 'rap' sessions" (*The University Bookman,* winter 1978).

The greatest indictment of modern education is that moral teachings and character training have been left out of the curriculum of public schools and universities. Under the guise of separation of church and state, the Bible, God's Word to mankind about *how to live*, is not open to discussion. It is lampooned, ridiculed and rejected, and viewed at best as merely "Hebrew and Greek literature."

Modern education has not helped stabilize masses of youth under assault by the media and the mass disintegration of families. Without the traditional influence of unified, proper families, including the guidance of both parents and all grandparents, children lack even the basic moral compass that guided previous generations. Education stoutly refuses to address moral training. Students in seminary schools and medical schools are taught to absorb the philosophy and practices, without question, of the system that is training them. To honestly question, or to demand *proof* of common *assumptions*, invites scorn and rejection. Loyalty to existing philosophy and the system in control is placed above integrity and ethics. In addition, there is an urgent need for almost 2 million more teachers just to stem overcrowding in American schools. What about the large standard size of many classrooms in other parts of the world?

The institutions producing the leaders of industry and society are poorly equipped to address the awesome challenges that face mankind. And, while the need has never been greater, real leaders with moral backbone have almost vanished. Soon, God-hating, law-hating, truth-hating legislators of this world will no longer be able to label God's Word as "hate literature" because it condemns perverse, immoral conduct. Modern education is now corrupting its last generation, and religion has done little or nothing to stop it!

Religion

Since the extended family no longer grounds, trains and supports youth, and modern education has failed to stand in the gap, it would seem that religion would fill the void. But it also has failed mankind for millennia. The world is deceived by *all* its forms of religion. *None* of the religions of the world have shown the way to peace, happiness, abundance and prosperity. *None* have solved humanity's problems!

Think of the so-called "great religions" of the world; Islam, Hinduism, Buddhism, Taoism, Judaism, Confucianism and Shinto. Even the most cursory review of the countries where they are practiced is a litany of the world's worst problems; ignorance, abject poverty, superstition, terrible degeneration, violence and civil war, resulting famine, disease, suffering, misery and despair. These could hardly be described as offering the promise of utopia, the coming of a better world. Rather, they are a picture, and even a study, of the awfulness of man's attempts to solve his own problems.

However, professing Christianity has most influenced the world! But *this* Christianity is a counterfeit, with teachings diametrically opposite those of its founder, Jesus Christ! For nearly 2,000 years, counterfeit Christianity has seduced most of the world. Its system is well-organized, well-established, and *appears* to be of God, with roots supposedly going back to the original apostles. Any counterfeit has to *appear* genuine to the average onlooker. This substitute Christianity, in fact, does; until one looks beyond the façade. But most never investigate below the surface.

Speaking of the fruits of this world's Christianity, as it has been affected by modern education, a Methodist bishop said, "We who are to overcome the world have been overcome by the world." Another senior religious leader said, "We churchmen are gifted at changing wine into water, watering down religion." How true!

The world is also deceived about how *false* Christianity has persecuted *true* Christianity, the Church where those preparing to rule with Christ are trained. Tens of thousands have been imprisoned, tortured and killed for practicing the true teachings of Christ. This is not God's world. It is cut off from Him and held hostage by an unseen *super-kidnapper*. All of mankind has been deceived into believing the soothing words of this great *captor*, thinking themselves better off under his care and leadership. I speak of Satan the devil and his hijacking, 6,000 years ago, of Adam and Eve and all the inhabitants of planet Earth ever after! The world has remained his *willing* captive.

Another Look At Democracy

We saw that in the end none of man's forms of government work either very well or for very long. Yet most democratic leaders believe that the spread of their form of government, democracy, is crucial to solving the world's problems and bringing freedom, abundance and happiness to all. Is this true?

The following shows the pattern of how democracies deteriorate. This astonishing quote, usually attributed to Alexander Tyler (circa late 1700s), pertains to the fall of the Athenian republic but applies to the ailing democracies of this modern age: "A democracy cannot exist as a permanent form of government. It can only exist until the voters discover that they can vote themselves money from the [public treasury]. From that moment on, the majority always votes for the candidates promising the most money from the [public treasury], with the result that a democracy always collapses over a loose fiscal policy followed by a dictatorship. The average age of the world's great civilizations has been two hundred years. These nations have progressed through the following sequence: from bondage to spiritual faith, from spiritual faith to great courage, from courage to liberty, from liberty to abundance, from abundance to selfishness, from selfishness to complacency, from complacency to apathy, from apathy to dependency, from dependency back to bondage."

If true, this means modern democracies will soon return to bondage. While all governments of men promise "pie in the sky," they are filled with graft, corruption, immorality and every form of deception. Most Americans saw this demonstrated in the 1990s from the highest offices in the country.

Man-Made Utopia Possible?

Do men possess the capacity to design and build a utopia? Considering the world's rapidly deteriorating condition, the question seems ridiculous. Understand. A man-made utopia is not in the making. Man's efforts to bring about such utopias have always failed. But we should still ask the question, and consider one such effort.

An English reformer, Robert Owen was internationally renowned for his amazing success in efficiently managing textile mills. In 1826, he came to the United States to conduct a social experiment in New Harmony, Indiana. He felt that by providing all able-bodied workers with challenging, fulfilling and enjoyable work, a utopian society would emerge. His community was carefully balanced between his textile mill, agriculture and various services. He attempted to cover all bases in this costly experiment.

Since Owen was hostile toward religion, he based his utopia solely on secular principles. He was also familiar with the ideas of Plato and other philosophers, and incorporated some into his own theory.

Owen's formula for utopia only considered physical requirements. It ignored spiritual and moral guidelines. As always, human nature appeared. Rivalries, friction and poor cooperation with associates plagued the experiment, forcing its abandonment within two years. Owen returned to England, concluding that human nature, and contentious human relations, blocked any hope of cooperation. While Owen recognized that human nature stood in the way, neither he nor any philosopher could find a formula to modify it.

Human philosophers may talk about utopia, but they cannot make it a reality. It is not within the power of men to bring peace, happiness, prosperity and all the good things of life.

The Great "Either/Or"

Many futurists believe that the world is accelerating toward a dizzying, kaleidoscopic array of constantly-improving, labor-saving devices, faster transportation, efficient forms of energy, better machines and endless forms of recreation and pleasure, and toward a reduced work week of three days!

They live in a dreamworld. Their ability to blind themselves to the hard, cold realities of the world around them is practically an art form. They have developed the "skill" of being able to ignore the grim truth of mankind's real plight, and replace it with the hoped-for world of the four "L's" of *liberty, leisure, luxury* and *license*!

While many may think they would enjoy a life of constant pleasure and leisure, others recognize that this would be a world filled with every conceivable form of escapism. Idleness and ease would be exposed as an enemy, instead of a friend. This is because many people who lack purpose for being and the fulfillment of production would turn to drugs, alcohol, and even worse decadence and immorality. And, with insurmountable problems facing vast segments of mankind, how could a few countries of the West enjoy a continually greater "lap of luxury," while the rest of the underdeveloped world remained content to live short, miserable lives, having lacked the barest necessities? How would this work? The world has grown too small for this to be remotely possible. There is no push-button dreamworld on the horizon, unless it is the danger of world leaders pushing buttons controlling the modern weapons of mass destruction, and the "dream" is man fulfilling his worst nightmare!

Today, more and more scientists and world leaders are concerned whether mankind *has* a future. They recognize the terrible potential of the world's worst weapons. And, as U.S. President George W. Bush said, "Increasingly, the world's worst weapons are becoming available to, and may fall into the hands of, the world's worst leaders." This dangerous reality is a truly frightening prospect!

Which picture is true? Famous philosopher, Aldous Huxley, expressed mankind's great "either/or" future this way: "Most prophecy tends to oscillate between an extreme of gloom and the wildest optimism! The world, according to one set of seers, is headed for disaster; according to the other, the world is destined, within a generation or two, to become a kind of gigantic Disneyland, in which the human race will find perpetual happiness playing with an endless assortment of ever more ingenious mechanical toys."

Science can put men on the moon but it is completely incapable of putting peace, happiness and prosperity on earth. These are all beyond its reach. The *plain truth* is that the stark reality of world conditions points toward gloom and disaster, not last-minute victory snatched from the jaws of defeat and credited to science. There *will* be a last-minute victory, but it will come from God instead of the very men who have brought near destruction upon themselves.

What Does God Say?

We have examined the opinions (and fruits) of men; religionists, scientists, educators, futurists and experts of every sort. None has, or ever will, hold the answers to the world's question of survival! Yet, if we *are* to survive, mankind's questions demand answers. We have seen that civilization cannot continue forever as it is. *Leaders* have defaulted their responsibility. *Religion* has remained spiritually bankrupt. *Education* now occurs in a moral vacuum. *Families* no longer provide even the most basic stability. The world's institutions are breaking down, exposing themselves as complete failures. Something *must* happen. Big changes have to occur. Reality thunders that worldwide calamity lies just over the horizon!

Of course, the great Creator God; who made the heavens, the earth and man; holds the answers. They are revealed in His Word. *This* is what we must examine. *This* is where we will find understanding. *This* is where we will learn how tomorrow's wonderful world, the true promised utopia, will come! But first we must deeply understand the ultimate CAUSE of this world's insoluble problems. We must learn WHY the world is in the terrible mess that it is!

Chapter II: The World's Problems, Evils & Ills

This world has terminal cancer. Every kind of tumor has spread throughout civilization's "body." Man's solution? Continually take "biopsies," then seek more and bigger band-aids to *cover* the tumors! Mankind has treated all the bad effects, and none of the causes. Again, every effect has a cause. Good effects flow from good causes. Bad effects can always be traced to bad causes.

A Great Unseen Law

Everyone understands the law of gravity. All recognize that if they break this law, it could "break" them. If one accidentally drops a brick on his foot, the result could be broken bones. If a skydiver jumps from an airplane, and the parachute fails to open, the result is certain death. There is no misunderstanding this.

Here are some examples that are only a little harder to understand, but are just as true:

- If a person is constantly sick, it is obvious that principles of health (proper diet, sufficient exercise and sleep, etc.) are being broken. Bad health has one or more causes.
- If a marriage ends in divorce, it can also be attributed to one or more causes: Lack of communication, financial woes, death of a child, sexual problems, unhappiness on the job, etc.
- If someone is arrested for drunk driving, it is not hard to see what *caused* the arrest.
- While most never identify cause and effect as a great law governing almost every action in life, they are at least somewhat aware that it is a general principle at work in certain circumstances.

Every effect can be traced to one or more causes. Unwanted or illegitimate pregnancies, crime, drug addiction, bankruptcy, and a thousand other effects, are all linked to specific causes. Create your own list. You may find it to be endless.

The King James Version of the Bible teaches, *"...the curse causeless shall not come"* (*Prov. 26:2*). Two other translations of this verse are *"... the undeserved curse will never hit its mark"* (Jerusalem Bible), and *"... the baseless curse never goes home"* (Moffatt). This scripture is saying that every effect carries a reason. There are no undeserved curses, there is a CAUSE for every EFFECT.

Why can man not see this law at work when he looks at the world as a whole? Why is it that no one is looking for the cause of this world's ills and evils? Why are educators not teaching this greatest of all principles? As you look at the world around you, are you concerned with it? Do you ever wonder *why* the world is filled with misery, unhappiness and discontent? Why have even those professing Christianity ignored this important relationship between cause and effect?

The cause of all the world's troubles began in the Garden of Eden, as simple as this sounds, it is true. The world has lost sight of a basic decision made by Adam and Eve. They chose not to eat of the tree of life, choosing instead to eat of the tree of the knowledge of good and evil. Have you ever wondered what would have happened if those two people had chosen the Tree of Life? Think of how this would have changed the entire world. *Everything* would be different!

There would be no armies, wars, death, devastation or displacement of peoples. There would be no famine or hunger, because there would be plenty of food for everyone. There would be few doctors, because there would be no illness. All of the hospitals and clinics would never have existed. Neither would the prisons, jails, judges, courts and police forces that exist to punish lawbreakers. Happiness, abundance, prosperity and peace would "break out" all over the world. All people would get along; neighbors, families, individuals and nations. Can you imagine such a world?

When Adam and Eve made the wrong decision almost six millennia ago, it directly affected *you* and *me*! They brought untold effects, because of their single wrong cause, and this has not been understood prior to the 20th Century. Let's examine the plain truth about WHY the world is in its current state of unending problems.

<u>What is the Cause?</u>

The Bible identifies the underlying root causes of why things go right or go wrong. It is the ultimate book explaining the law of cause and effect! It also reveals *how* to address wrong causes. It is the source to which we must look to see why this world *must* and will be replaced by tomorrow's wonderful world!

Human troubles and evils are prophesied to grow much, MUCH worse in this age. Appalling violence, terrorism and war are escalating as human nature hurtles further out of control. After a recent school shooting where many lay slaughtered, a parent remarked, "I don't understand this world anymore." You *can* understand both this world and the cause of its troubles. Understanding human nature is the all-important key.

The Bible teaches that there are two different and opposing ways of life. One is best described as the "GIVE" way, the other is the way of "GET." The *give* way is outgoing, outflowing concern for the needs, concerns and welfare of others. It is focused away from the self. It is diametrically opposite thinking from the *get* way, which is incoming, focused on self, with one's own interests and needs at heart.

The Bible teaches that God has a "divine nature" (*II Peter 1:4*). This nature is "natural" to God, but it is *not* natural for people. God practices the give way of life (*James 1:17*), but human beings practice the opposite. Though most will never admit it, they are almost totally preoccupied with getting, accumulating, satisfying, and focusing on the *self*! All human beings possess human nature. The selfishness, rottenness, violence and terrible evils that spring from human nature have plagued the world for thousands of years. The apostle John said, *"The whole world lies in wickedness"* (*I John 5:19*). The cause of this condition lies directly at the feet of evil human nature.

Every "expert" has a different opinion about *what* human nature is and *where* it comes from. None understand the answers to these questions or the question of *why* human nature exists. This is because they reject the source to understanding the answers to *all* of life's greatest questions.

Consider the paradox! Think of all the wonderful things the human mind is capable of producing. Its ingenuity and inventiveness are practically limitless. Yet it cannot solve the most basic of life's great problems: poverty, ignorance, immorality, crime, war and misery. All of these are byproducts of unbridled human nature, which also comes from the human mind, or does it?

No "Better Nature"

Many theologians and religionists teach that all humans are endowed with a "better nature" hiding inside, waiting to be found, tapped and used. This is untrue. The Bible says no such thing! Yet millions subscribe to it.

In *Mark 7: 20-23* Christ addressed and described human nature: *"And He said, That which comes out of the man, that defiles the man. For from within, out of the heart of men, proceed evil thoughts, adulteries, fornications, murders, thefts, covetousness, wickedness, deceit, lasciviousness, an evil eye, blasphemy, pride, foolishness: All these evil things come from within, and defile the man"*

First, accept that Christ made this statement, and as such it must be true. This is a staggering understanding. The prophet Jeremiah added, *"The heart is deceitful above all things, and desperately wicked: who can know it?"* (*Jeremiah 17:9*). Most do not see this in themselves, though they readily see it in others. Further, the apostle Paul wrote, *"the carnal [natural] mind is enmity [hostile] against God: for it is not subject to the law of God, neither indeed can be"* (*Romans 8:7*).

These are incredible statements about the minds of *all* human beings. But how did the torrent of evil thoughts, which pour from all people, come to exist in them in the first place? How did it get there?

The Arch Broadcaster

Does God infuse human nature into tiny babies at birth? Does an all-wise, all-powerful, loving God take innocent children and turn them toward terrible evil from the moment they are born? And, if God does not put this nature there, where does it come from?

Paul wrote the Ephesian Church about the life that God had called them out of when He revealed His truth to them. *Ephesians 2:2* references the power of the devil and his influence upon the world: *"Wherein in time past you walked according to the course of this world, according to the prince of the power of the air, the spirit that now works in the children of disobedience."*

This is an incredible verse. The phrase *"children of disobedience"* is also found in *Ephesians 5:6* and *Colossians 3:6*. Let's examine how these references relate to the phrase, *"prince of the power of the air."*

Notice that *verse 2* states Satan's spirit *"...works in the children of disobedience."* Do you see this? Do you grasp it? Satan has the power to use the "air" to broadcast, through his spirit, an attitude of disobedience!

34

His spirit sends moods, feelings and attitudes of hostility into people's minds. These work within people's hearts and minds, bringing disobedience. This "air power" gives the devil great influence, allowing him to send thoughts of confusion, deceit, anger, pride, hate, foolishness, vanity, jealousy, lust, greed, envy and much more directly into people's thinking!

Think of it this way. The devil owns a powerful radio station, broadcasting 24 hours a day. Since *Revelation 12:9* states that he *"deceives the whole world,"* this mighty station reaches and deceives all civilization! Yet, his incredible cunning has even been able to convince most that he does not exist!

The devil is far more powerful than most realize. The Bible identifies him as this world's god. Notice what Paul wrote to the Corinthians: *"In whom the god of this world has blinded the minds of them which believe not, lest the light of the glorious gospel of Christ, who is the image of God, should shine unto them"* (*II Corinthians 4:4*). Only one with enormous power to influence, as a virtual "god" could blind and deceive on a scale so staggering. As a result, he has produced a world filled with disobedience (*I John 5:19*).

On the other hand, a Christian follows God and obeys His Law. Paul recorded that God has a spiritual Law that is holy, just and good (*Romans 7:12, 14*). This law summarizes the give way of life. Christians obey it. But how do they do this? In *Acts 5:32*, the apostle Peter referred to *"the Holy Spirit, [which] God has given to them that obey Him."* Christians understand and practice obedience to God, not disobedience. God's Spirit is given upon repentance and baptism (*Acts 2:38*). This Spirit helps Christians obey His Law.

Before the invention of radio, Satan's power, as arch broadcaster and prince of the power of the air, could not be as easily understood. But now it can. We can now better understand the *"children of disobedience."* Like Christians, these people are inspired and guided by a spirit, that of the god of this world. Satan broadcasts a spirit of disobedience, through attitudes, into humanity. *Ephesians 2:2* is plain, but a deceived world knows nothing of this understanding.

If you listen to the radio, you usually pick a station that plays what you want to hear. Today, people "surf" radio or television stations. Eventually something interests them, and they stop and listen to a station of their choosing. In every case, stations are selected by choice. People have control over what they hear or watch. It is not the same with Satan's radio station. The world, including you, does not decide to tune into the devil's broadcast. And no one ever sets out to be deceived. But every human being on earth is automatically tuned to Satan's wavelength! His wickedness, hostility, rebellion, deceit and selfishness are continually "on the air."

Therefore, it is really Satan's nature that is being labeled as human nature. In fact, once it is injected into people, Satan's nature becomes *natural* to them. It becomes *their* nature, now *human* nature. But he cannot force minds to yield to his attitudes; they must *allow* his thoughts to enter. Though you cannot see it, anymore than you can see radio waves or television signals, the air around you is literally charged and "crackles" with the power and energy of Satan's broadcast.

It is absolutely critical to understand how this spirit works in people. It is the single greatest key to understanding exactly how Satan can deceive and manipulate over *six billion* people.

An Important Illustration

Before further examining the devil's role and how he came to be as he is, consider this illustration. It demonstrates how Satan can influence and sway humanity through his broadcast.

The setting involves King Cyrus of Persia. God wanted him to return to Jerusalem and build a second temple to replace Solomon's, which had been destroyed. Here is how God communicated to Cyrus: *"Now in the first year of Cyrus king of Persia, that the word of the Lord by the mouth of Jeremiah might be fulfilled, the Lord stirred up the spirit of Cyrus king of Persia, that he made a proclamation throughout all his kingdom, and put it also in writing" (Ezra 1:1).*

God was able to communicate with Cyrus by "stirring up" his *spirit*. Satan does the same thing. He works directly with the human spirit, which gives the human brain the power of *intellect* beyond that of animal *instinct*. Just as God can lead a human being toward a *right purpose*, Satan's spirit influences people toward hate, anger, selfishness, violence, competition, vanity, jealousy, lust, greed, murder and deceit.

Of course, when Satan injects his attitudes into an unsuspecting mankind, it has no idea that he is doing it. The devil does not announce his intentions in advance or speak aloud in an audible voice; he is far cleverer than this.

Murder, Lies and Destruction

Just as God the Father has children, Satan is also a father with children. Notice, a confrontation between Christ and people who professed to *"believe on Him"* occurred in *John 8:30-31*. You should read the entire account, but here is a summary. Those who professed belief in Christ actually sought to kill Him (*vs. 37*). Christ said, *"But you seek to kill Me, because My word has no place in you."* He further added, *"But now you seek to kill Me, a Man that has told you the truth"* (*vs. 40*). Many *say* they want to hear the truth, but not if it means being told that they are wrong. This account comes to a remarkable climax in *verses 43-44*. Christ asked, *"Why do you not understand My speech?"* He answers His own question with, *"...because you cannot hear My word."* Verse 44 explains, *"You are of your father the devil, and the lusts of your father you will do. He was a murderer from the beginning, and abode not in the truth, because there is no truth in him. When he speaks a lie, he speaks of his own: for he is a liar, and the father of it."* Christ plainly said, *"You are not of God"* (*vs. 47*), and these devil-inspired religious leaders immediately accused Him of *"having a demon"* (*vs. 48*)! Many today who profess to "believe on Christ" are no different than those described here.

This is a powerful statement. The devil is a father who kills, deceives and destroys (*Rev. 9:11*). As the author of murder, lies and destruction, he broadcasts these attitudes to his children around the world!

The Devil Holds Sway Over Earth

Make no mistake! The world is filled with the children of the devil. It has been observed that children are basically much like their parents. Therefore, Satan's children lie, hate, murder and destroy. Look at the world. It should be clear *why* confusion, war, ignorance, poverty, disease and misery abound among the nations. The fruits of human nature, *Satan's* nature, are evident everywhere.

Notice Paul's description of the "last days" preceding Christ's Return: *"This know also, that in the last days perilous [dangerous] times shall come. For men shall be lovers of their own selves, covetous, boasters, proud, blasphemers, disobedient to parents, unthankful, unholy, without natural affection, trucebreakers, false accusers, incontinent, fierce, despisers of those that are good, traitors, heady, highminded, lovers of pleasures more than lovers of God; having a form of godliness, but denying the power thereof: from such turn away"* (II Tim. 3:1-5).

While the world is *filled* with religion, *"a form of godliness"*, it is neither the truth nor the religion of God. It denies the power of the true God, and the world unwittingly worships a different being, one who palms himself off as the God of the Bible.

Recall, the devil is called the *"god of this world"* (II Cor. 4:4). He is also called the *"prince of this world"* (John 12:31; 14:30; 16:11) and *"prince of the power of the air"* (Eph. 2:2). And remember, John wrote that he *"deceives the whole world"* (Rev. 12:9). This includes you! But you were not *born* with human nature any more than you were born with the Holy Spirit already in your mind. Human nature, like God's Spirit, is acquired.

Lucifer's Rebellion

But how did Satan come to have his spirit, his *attitude*? The Bible identifies the devil as the former archangel known as Lucifer. Let's read of Lucifer *after* he had become Satan. *Isaiah 14:12-15* gives many clues about where Lucifer was once located, what he did and what happened to him. Read carefully and notice the key phrases: *"How are you fallen from heaven, O Lucifer, son of the morning! How are you cut down to the ground, which did weaken the nations! For you have said in your heart, I will ascend into heaven, I will exalt my throne above the stars of God: I will sit also upon the mount of the congregation, in the sides of the north: I will ascend above the heights of the clouds; I will be like the Most High. Yet you shall be brought down to hell [the "grave", see verses 9 and 11], to the sides of the pit."*

- Only the devil *"weakens the nations"* and said he would *"ascend unto heaven."* No *man* fits this description, having a throne that can be put above the *"stars of heaven."*
- *Ezekiel 28:12-17* adds important information and parallels *Isaiah 14.* It speaks of one who *"seals up the sum, full of wisdom, and perfect in beauty,"* who had also *"been in Eden the garden of God."* No human has ever been perfect, and Satan the devil was

the serpent who beguiled Eve in the Garden of Eden.
- *Verse 13* states, *"you were created."* Satan is a created being.
- *Verse 14* calls him *"the cherub that covers."* Exodus 25:17-20 describes the remaining two faithful *"cherubs that cover[ed]"* God's throne in the Old Testament tabernacle, where their wings cover the *"mercy seat."*
- The latter part of *Ezekiel 28:14* says this *"king"* was *"upon the holy mountain of God"* and *"walked...in the midst of the stones of fire."* This describes the area around God's throne.
- *Verse 15* states, *"till iniquity [lawlessness] was found in you,"* and *verse 16* refers to it as *"sin."*
- *Verse 16* also describes this cherub as having been *"cast...out of"* heaven. God also said He would *"destroy"* (Hebrew: expel) Lucifer from heaven.
- *Verse 17* reveals that his *"heart was lifted up because of [his] beauty,"* and that his wisdom was *"corrupted...by reason of [his] brightness."* The verse ends with God casting him down *"to the ground,"* where the kings of the earth *"behold him."*

Lucifer was a brilliant being, an *"angel of light"* (*II Cor. 11:13-15*). *Lucifer* means *"the light bringer."* This formerly brilliant, wise, perfect being once brought *great light* to all who were around him. But he rebelled, sinned, thus becoming the *"prince of darkness."* His rebellion turned him into a twisted, perverted being. While of great intelligence, he has literally become an insane, *fallen* angel who no longer understands right from wrong. He believes he is right and God is wrong. Hate, anger, bitterness, murder, deceit, vanity, pride, envy and resentment entered him. These are the attitudes that Satan broadcasts, into an unsuspecting humanity! We will learn how mankind opened the door to Satan's wavelength.

The Creation of Man and Adam's Choice

The book of Genesis describes the creation of man. It means the book of *beginnings* and covers a period of over 2,000 years. However, it is not written to show detail. Rather, it represents a look at the most important *high points* of human history. The creation week and the time immediately following it are described in the first three chapters. Let's examine the creation of man and what God said about His "product" after it was finished.

- In *chapter 1*, God said, *"Let us [more than one] make man in our image, after our likeness" (vs. 26).* There was clearly more than one person involved in the creation of man.
- *Verse 25* shows that each animal was made after *"his kind."* Notice: *"And God made the beast of the earth after his kind, and cattle after their kind, and every thing that creeps upon the earth after his kind: and God saw that it was good."*
- *Verse 27* continues, *"So God created man in His own image, in the image of God created He him; male and female created He them."* This verse is a vital key to understanding that God's very purpose is to reproduce Himself. The human family and human reproduction is a type of this plan.
- *Verse 28* begins with an important statement: *"And God blessed them, and God said unto them, Be fruitful, and multiply, and replenish the earth."* If God had instilled evil, selfish, sinful human nature into Adam and Eve at the moment of their creation, it could hardly be described as "blessing" them. If this were the case, it would be better described as a curse.
- The *Genesis 1* account concludes with vitally important *verse 31:* *"And God saw everything that He had made, and, behold, it was very good."*
- Think about what this scripture is saying. In one sense, it is a stunning statement about human nature. Human nature is *not* very good, it is VERY EVIL. Yet God called His creation "very good."

If God *"blessed"* this couple and said that their creation was *"very good,"* then deceit (*Jeremiah*), hostility toward God's law (*Romans 8:7*), hate, selfishness, pride, vanity, lust and all the other evils of human nature (*Mark 7:20-23*) could not be present. There is no evidence of rebellion against God in this account. Therefore, it describes Adam and Eve *prior* to their encounter with Satan.

In *chapter 2*, God presented Adam and Eve with the choice that they would face (*chapter 3*) between the Tree of Life and the "tree of the knowledge of good and evil." They were offered the opportunity to decide between God's *"divine nature"* (*II Pet. 1:4*), building and developing *His* character, or taking on Satan's sinful nature. If Adam would have been willing to obey God's instruction, he could have qualified to replace Satan and restore the government of God on earth. Recall, Satan had rebelled and overthrown God's government on the earth.

But how did the devil gain access to mankind? What opened the door to his influence, to his broadcast? The well known but little understood Garden of Eden account of Adam and Eve eating the forbidden fruit holds the key (*Gen. 3:1-7*). This account represents a critical decision. Instead of following God's instruction, Adam took of the "tree of the knowledge of good and evil." He thought he knew better than God. He took *to himself* the right to decide between what was right (good) and what was wrong (evil). He thought that he could trust his own physical senses. In this sense, this decision did *"open his eyes"* (*vs. 7*), but not to the things of God, which come only by receiving God's Spirit (*I Cor. 2:9-10*). Certainly, God's Spirit did *not* enter them at this moment. The spirit of rebellion entered their minds for the first time. The evil spirit of Satan's influence was injected into their minds *at that moment* as the very first appearance of "human nature." This is how their *"eyes were opened."*

Adam's decision precluded any opportunity to acquire *spiritual* knowledge from God. Thus, his understanding remained limited to what he could learn through the five physical senses, and left him open to Satan's broadcast. Human nature came into being for the first time. With this decision, Adam completely cut himself and mankind off from access to God. This other tree has been guiding the thinking of the men and nations of the world ever since Adam's fateful choice. For his great sin of rejecting God and the Tree of Life, Adam was rejected by God and cast from the garden. Mankind was cast out with him into Satan's world!

Satan lied to Eve, who led Adam into sin with her. He got them to reject, to disbelieve, what God had taught them in *Genesis 2:16-17*. The devil's deceit brought these two adult children to believe that they no longer needed to listen to God. Human nature entered. Being thrust from the garden, they were forced to fend for themselves. They rejected God's perfect Law (*Romans 7:12, 14*) and rule; His government over all creation, as guides in their lives, and yielded to Satan and his way of sin (*Romans 8:7; II Timothy. 2:26*). Because of sin, they no longer had access to God's blessings, guidance, protection or the gift of His Holy Spirit, which would have come by eating of the Tree of Life.

Human Nature is Not Inherited

Human nature did not come from God, but rather from Satan. So it is not inherited, it is acquired! A parent who loses an eye, a hand or a leg does not produce children with one eye, one hand or one leg. When God used one of Adam's ribs to create Eve, it did not mean that all men ever after lack one rib. The Bible refers to their son Abel as "righteous Abel." Their disobedience did not prevent his obedience.

Adam and Eve were adult "babies." Like babies born today, they were pure at the time of their creation ("birth"), but were quickly exposed to a "broadcast" they could not resist. Perhaps only days old, they could not discern right from wrong. Like most children, Adam and Eve chose not to listen to their parent, God. Instead, they believed Satan's lie that they would not "surely die." In so doing, they rejected the rule of the government of God in their lives. Again, if Adam had obeyed God's instruction, he could have qualified to replace Satan and restore the government of God on earth.

Let's examine one important New Testament instruction and example of how human nature is acquired, not inherited. Paul shed important light in the following warning that he issued to the Corinthian Church: *"For I am jealous over you with godly jealousy: for I have espoused you to one husband, that I may present you as a chaste virgin to Christ. But I fear, lest by any means, as the serpent beguiled Eve through his subtlety, so your minds should be corrupted from the simplicity that is in Christ"* (II Cor. 11:2-3).

Paul was writing to people who lived 4,000 years after Adam and Eve. He knew that the devil was still alive and active. The Corinthians were adults capable of being deceived ("beguiled") in the same way as Eve. Paul warned them to be on guard that they not return to following the ways of human nature. Just as Eve's nature was not evil and hostile to God before she was deceived, neither was the nature of the converted Corinthians. Once a person is called and converted, having received the Spirit of God, he has put off the old human nature of his past life. Paul also added in *Ephesians 2:3, "Among whom also we all had our conversation in times past in the lusts of our flesh, fulfilling the desires of the flesh and of the mind; and were by nature the children of wrath, even as others."* These verses follow and are part of the scripture referencing Satan as the *"prince of the power of the air."*

It would be grossly unfair of God to inject newborn babies with human nature and place them under His wrath. Do you see this point? Human nature is acquired, then stirs people to disobedience (sin), and this puts them under the wrath of God. Most simply drift along in life, following whatever impulses and ideas ("imaginations") strike them from moment to moment. All of *Ephesians 1* is Paul's recounting to those brethren about their calling into God's way of life, and *chapter 2* describes their "*dis*-acquiring" human nature.

Conversion Changes Human Nature

Most people have absolutely no idea why they were born! This is spiritually revealed knowledge, unattainable to all whom God has not called to understand His truth (*John 6:44, 65*). Lucifer rebelled and became Satan. He sought to overthrow the government of God, and disqualified himself to remain part of it. Each human being that God calls is presented with the same choice; *yielding to God and His government or yielding to Satan and his nature.*

God is a Father who now has one Spirit composed Son, but who will later have many more sons (*Romans 8:19; Hebrews 2:10*). He is reproducing Himself by developing His character in yielded, conquered, spirit-begotten human beings. God begets His children spiritually, as do human fathers physically. The Spirit-led children of God slowly take on the spiritual likeness of God, in "divine" nature (*II Peter 1:4*) and holy, righteous character. Peter described Christians as *"partakers of the divine nature"*, the nature of God. There is the physical nature of creation, human nature and God's nature. God is re-fashioning corrupt, carnal human nature into wonderful, glorious, perfect, holy spiritual character, His nature!

Character is understanding, knowing, right from wrong and doing what is right instead of what is wrong. God reveals what is right, but righteous character is built through the power of free moral agency; deciding to do what is right. God has perfect character in every respect. God is love. Love is the fulfilling of the law (*Romans 13:10*), which requires yielding to God. It is outgoing, out flowing concern for others, putting them first; ahead of the interests of self.

Satan's nature is selfish, incoming and concerned only with what is best for self and how to get more for self. When over 6 billion people are living this way, the results are absolutely catastrophic for the world as a whole. Nothing will change until human nature is banished from earth!

Christ Restores God's Government—Utopia Begins!

Throughout His ministry, Christ announced that He would return and establish the kingdom of God on the earth. He will be crowned as King of kings and Lord of lords (*Revelations*). After His Resurrection, He assumed His position at the throne of God, which governs the universe (*Luke 19:12-27; Acts 1:9-11; Hebrews 1:3; 8:1; 10:12*). But, upon His Return, He will open eternal life and salvation to the whole world. The world is now cut off from God (*Isaiah 59:1-2*), blinded and led by Satan's nature.

When Christ returns, He actually brings a restoration of God's way of life to earth. Here is how Peter described this event: *"Repent you therefore, and be converted, that your sins may be blotted out, when the times of refreshing shall come from the presence of the Lord; And He shall send Jesus Christ, which before was preached unto you: Whom the heaven must receive until the times of restitution [restoration] of all things..."* (*Acts 3:19-21*). The government of God will soon be restored to earth. The peoples of all nations will sit before Christ on His throne.

Notice again that some will have qualified to rule and some will not: *"When the Son of Man shall come in His glory, and all the holy angels with Him, then shall He sit upon the throne of His glory: And before Him shall be gathered all nations: and He shall separate them one from another, as a shepherd divides his sheep from the goats: And He shall set the sheep on His right hand, but the goats on the left. Then shall the King say unto them on His right hand, Come, you blessed of My Father, inherit the kingdom prepared for you [all who have overcome] from the foundation of the world"* (*Matthew 25:31-34*).

Only those who truly submitted to God and successfully resisted Satan throughout their lives will take part in this glorious future. Notice: *"He that overcomes shall inherit all things; and I will be his God, and he shall be My son. But the fearful, and unbelieving, and the abominable, and murderers, and whoremongers, and sorcerers, and idolaters, and all liars, shall have their part in the lake which burns with fire and brimstone: which is the second death"* (*Revelations. 21:7-8*). Could you be one who inherits all things in God's kingdom?

Nations Reject Christ at His Return!

Seven trumpet plagues precede Christ's Return. *Revelation 11* describes the blowing of the seventh trumpet, and what it means for all nations. Notice John's description of this wonderful moment and what it signifies; and how the single greatest event in world history is fulfilled: *"And the seventh angel sounded [his trumpet]; and there were great voices in heaven, saying, The kingdoms of this world are become the kingdoms of our Lord, and of His Christ; and He shall reign forever and ever..." (vs. 15).*

Christ comes again (*John 14:3*), returning in the clouds (*Matthew 24:30; Acts 1:9-11*). This is the precise moment when the saints are resurrected (*I Thessalonians 4:14-17; I Corinthians 15:52*), and stand with Christ on the Mount of Olives (*Zechariah 14:4-5*). It is when the prophets receive their reward (*Luke 13:28*). The saints then begin their rule over all nations (*Daniel 7:22*).

This astonishing prophecy carries other enormous implications. It is the beginning of Christ's purpose to expand His Plan beyond the few called and trained during the last 6,000 years. Surely this brings great joy and exultation on earth! Surely all nations are thrilled at the prospect of being governed by Christ. Right?

Return to *Revelation 11*: *"And the nations were angry, and Your wrath is come, and the time of the dead, that they should be judged, and that You should give reward unto Your servants the prophets, and to the saints, and them that fear Your name, small and great; and should destroy them which destroy the earth" (vs. 18)*. This prophecy reveals that the nations of earth will not be happy, because they will not be ready for, nor will they understand, what is happening. Raw human nature will explode into the open. Enormous armies will actually try to attack and destroy Jesus Christ (*Revelations 17:14*). They will have been taught, even programmed to believe, that the real Christ is the *Anti-Christ*! This will result in a final climactic battle near Jerusalem (*Zechariah 14:1-2*).

Notice *Zechariah 14:3*: *"Then shall the Lord go forth, and fight against those nations, as when He fought in the day of battle"* completely defeating them; *Zechariah 14:4* states that *"His feet shall stand in that day upon the mount of Olives"* both *Matthew 25:31* and *Revelation 17:14* show that a spirit army will assist Christ in this battle. Now read *Revelation 17:14*: *"These shall make war with the Lamb, and the Lamb shall overcome them: for He is Lord of lords, and King of kings: and they that are with Him are called, and chosen, and faithful."*

What happens next? Here is how *Zechariah 14:12* describes the battle: *"And this shall be the plague wherewith the Lord will smite all the people that have fought against Jerusalem; their flesh shall consume away while they stand upon their feet, and their eyes shall consume away in their holes, and their tongue shall consume away in their mouth."* This will be a very short battle. Christ's enemies will literally rot while standing, before they can fall down. What a horrible scene results when human nature turns on Christ. Yet the awesome power of God crushes all rebellion on earth. There will be no "high-level negotiations" about how, whether and when Christ takes office.

How could the world be so ignorant of God's Plan that they turn and fight Christ? Understand. The ministers of professing Christianity have utterly failed to teach the peoples of the world (*Matthew 28:19-20*) God's precious truth, and that His world-ruling government is coming. They have deceived and deluded the masses with false doctrines and misunderstanding of God's supreme purpose! They have directly contributed to the mess that the world is in. The entirety of *Ezekiel 34* describes the history of this world's collective "ministry" and how it serves itself while claiming to represent and serve God. This chapter concludes with a description of how King David will be resurrected and placed over the tribes of Israel in their stead. However, a deceived, ignorant world will be completely confused at Christ's Return, not recognizing that He is about to impose, literally force, peace upon all nations.

Satan to be Banished!

When Christ returns, Satan, as the deposed ruler over earth, will be removed. No leader can replace a disqualified leader and permit him to remain and co-rule with him. The disqualified leader would second-guess and undermine all that the new leader plans to change and implement. He would seek to influence the masses until he could bring about an overthrow of the government to reinstall himself, without power-sharing. If human governments understand this, certainly God does. He knows that Satan must be removed from his position of influence.

Revelation 20 describes the establishing of Christ's 1,000-year reign with the saints. Now understand one of the very first actions necessary to begin the true peace process for earth's inhabitants: *"And I saw an angel come down from heaven, having the key of the bottomless pit and a great chain in his hand. And he laid hold on the dragon, that old serpent, which is the Devil, and Satan, and bound him a thousand years, and cast him into the bottomless pit, and shut him up, and set a seal upon him, that he should deceive the nations no more, till the thousand years should be fulfilled: and after that he must be loosed a little season" (vs. 1-3).*

This verse contains crucial understanding about God's future plan for all mankind. Soon, Satan will be bound (imprisoned) and rendered unable to deceive the inhabitants of earth. The temptations of this world and human nature, caused by Satan, will disappear. Though there will still be certain fleshly pulls that all will have to overcome (*Romans 7:18, 21-23*), the devil's radio station will be closed down.

When Satan is bound, peace will literally explode forth all over the world. The saints will be ruling with Christ from Jerusalem, having restored the government of God in His kingdom, administered by the God Family. God's *"holy, just, perfect and spiritual"* Law (*Romans 7:12-14*) will be enforced among all nations.

Human Nature Will Slowly Disappear Worldwide

Human nature will not instantly disappear, but, with mankind no longer deceived and the scales of blindness now covering the eyes of humanity removed (*Isaiah. 25:7*). People will begin to see the truth in a way never before possible. Old habits die hard. Billions will have to unlearn attitudes and thought patterns that have been natural to everyone for a lifetime. It will not be easy, but it will occur relatively quickly.

The influence of Satan, through high government offices, has been far greater than most could dream. Notice what Paul wrote: *"Finally, my brethren, be strong in the Lord, and in the power of His might. Put on the whole armor of God, that you may be able to stand against the wiles of the devil. For we wrestle not against flesh and blood, but against principalities, against powers, against the rulers of the darkness of this world, against spiritual wickedness [Greek: wicked spirits] in high places" (Ephesians 6:10-12).*

Many New Testament scriptures describe the extent to which human nature, unchecked by overcoming, has complete dominance over every aspect of people's lives. And the fruits of human nature are evident around the world. Carefully consider and think about the following four extensive scriptures. Reflect on the evidence of them in people's lives. Paul wrote the Galatians, *"Now the works of the flesh are manifest [obvious], which are these; adultery, fornication, uncleanness, lasciviousness, idolatry, witchcraft, hatred, variance, emulations, wrath, strife, seditions, heresies, envyings, murders, drunkenness, revellings, and such like...they which do such things shall not inherit the kingdom of God"* (*Galatians 5:19-21*).

Now consider these next two extensive passages from Paul to the Romans: *"And even as they did not like to retain God in their knowledge, God gave them over to a reprobate mind, to do those things which are not convenient; being filled with all unrighteousness, fornication, wickedness, covetousness, maliciousness; full of envy, murder, debate, deceit, malignity; whisperers, backbiters, haters of God, despiteful, proud, boasters, inventors of evil things, disobedient to parents, without understanding, covenant breakers, without natural affection, implacable, unmerciful: who knowing the judgment of God, that they which commit such things are worthy of death, not only do the same, but have pleasure in them that do them"* (*Romans 1:28-32*).

This powerful list of wrong attitudes and wrong conduct summarizes the condition of all humanity. They will slowly disappear in a world without Satan. *"When I consider Your heavens, the work of Your fingers, the moon and the stars, which You have ordained"* (*Psalm 8:3*) and *"For such as be blessed of Him shall inherit the earth"* (*Psalm 37:22*).

Paul also wrote of an entire world under the influence and sway of the devil: *"There is none righteous, no, not one: There is none that understands, there is none that seeks after God. They are all gone out of the way, they are together become unprofitable; there is none that does good, no, not one. Their throat is an open sepulcher; with their tongues they have used deceit; the poison of asps is under their lips: Whose mouth is full of cursing and bitterness: Their feet are swift to shed blood: Destruction and misery are in their ways"* (*Romans 3:10-16*).

No wonder John commanded true Christians of all eras in the following direct way: *"Love not the world, neither the things that are in the world. If any man love the world, the love of the Father is not in him. For all that is in the world, the lust of the flesh, and the lust of the eyes, and the pride of life, is not of the Father, but is of the world"* (*I John 2:15-16*).

Imagine a world where all these kinds of evil behavior disappear. It is almost too wonderful to contemplate, but it will happen. The process of re-educating a civilization no longer deceived will spread around the world, encompassing all nations (*Isaiah 2:1-4*), and flowing from Jerusalem. The Holy Spirit, bringing fullness of understanding, will be available to all people.

THIS TIME IS COMING...AND SOON!

Chapter III: The Government In Tomorrow's World

Imagine a world where all false gods have been exposed for what they are, then removed and destroyed. Then imagine the entire world worshipping the true God. Picture the end of all wars, and all forms of violence and hate, which spring from the human heart. Now envision all marriages being happy for life, and with never a concern about adultery. Then, what if all children obeyed and honored their parents, who were teaching them God's way from birth? Try to picture never being told anything but the truth and the complete disappearance of all forms of dishonesty. This means also imagining a world without locks, keys, security systems and bank vaults, where nothing ever needed to be kept in a safe. What if there was no sickness or illness of any kind? What if all people enjoyed perfect, robust health?

Now envision a world of beauty and cleanliness, with no urban blight or slums, and no portions of humanity becoming degenerate or backward because of religious superstition, poor diet or illiteracy. Everyone would be concerned with *giving* instead of *getting*, which would ensure that all people had more than enough for themselves. What an incredible world this would be!

One World Government Necessary

For all these things to be possible, the world would require one super-government to enforce them. The nearly 200 sovereign, disagreeing, competing, warring and fighting governments of this society; in their numerous different forms and shapes; could never bring this to pass. If they could, it would have happened by now.

Man has been sentenced to 6,000 years of trying his own governments. The result? He has proven himself completely incapable of successfully governing even a single nation. Not one nation stands out in history as a beacon of success. If there were it would still exist on earth today, having shown itself capable of bringing peace, real happiness, security and abundance for all its citizens for hundreds or thousands of years. And then all other nations would have sought to copy its success; and all nations would now be modeled after it.

But this has not happened. The reason is that all of the conditions just described are only possible if they are FORCED upon a resistant mankind, now unwilling and unable to bring these things to itself. Yet here is what former British Prime Minister Clemet Attlee once acknowledged: "The world needs the consummation of our conception of world organization through world law if civilization is to survive!…We have not an awful lot of time. There is too much dangerous stuff in the world, and there are too many fools about, trigger-happy idiots and the like." Sir Winston Churchill also said this: "The creation of an authoritative all-powerful world order is the ultimate aim toward which we must strive. Unless some effective world super-government can be brought quickly into action, the proposals for peace and human progress are dark and doubtful." But, would any accept a single world government?

When God began to call me, I had applied to attend the United States Naval Academy, and an interview with my Congressman was a required part of the process. I had been learning about God's prophesied, world-ruling, super-government to be established by Christ at His Return. With this in mind, I asked Congressman McCullough his opinion of one world government, if it were in the hands of men. His answer was immediate and emphatic, "I do not believe it would work, but if I did I would be out shouting it from the housetops." Then he stated various objections. This experience made a lasting impression on me. Interestingly, I received the appointment (though I declined in favor of attending Ambassador College) because my Congressman told me that my question about world government had so intrigued him that it tipped the scales in my favor. He had simply never considered this great question before.

Since that time, many have suggested that one world government is the only way to world peace and stability. But many questions arise: Who would bring it? How would it be phased in? What laws would it administer? How would they be enforced? Would sovereign nations relinquish their authority to it? Would it succeed, or would it eventually oppress and enslave all mankind? These questions always stop thinkers, planners, leaders and scientists in their tracks. Therefore, solving mankind's great problems remains as elusive as ever. Everyone yearns for solutions, but no one knows how to obtain them. Why can experienced leaders and intelligent thinkers not find the answers? People understand that the only solution for mankind is one world government. Yet, at the same time, they acknowledge that this is utterly impossible if left in the hands of men. We are left with the conclusion that world government is necessary to save man from himself, and to save the planet from man!

World Government is Coming

We have seen that Christ will return to rule with the saints. Notice how it will encompass all peoples and nations: *"And in the days of these kings shall the God of heaven set up a kingdom, which shall never be destroyed: and the kingdom shall not be left to other people, but it shall break in pieces and consume all these kingdoms, and it shall stand forever"* (*Daniel 2:44*).

Have you ever read this scripture? It has always been in the Bible! Before His Return, God officially grants Christ authority to rule the world. *Daniel 7:14* states, *"And there was given Him dominion, and glory, and a kingdom, that all people, nations, and languages, should serve Him: His dominion is an everlasting dominion, which shall not pass away, and His kingdom that which shall not be destroyed."*

No wonder that, when Christ was on trial for His life, He said, *"My kingdom is not of this world: if My kingdom were of this world, then would My servants fight, that I should not be delivered to the Jews: but now is My kingdom not from here"* (*John 18:36*). Pilate had asked Him, *"Are you a king then?"* Christ answered, *"To this end was I born, and for this cause came I into the world..."* (*vs. 37*). Jesus knew that He was born to rule (*Luke 1:31-33*).

Here is how Isaiah described the scope and certainty of Christ's rule as He brings the government of God to earth. Savor and believe these words: *"For unto us a child is born, unto us a son is given: and the government shall be upon His shoulder: and His name shall be called Wonderful, Counselor, The mighty God, The everlasting Father, The Prince of Peace. Of the increase of His government and peace there shall be no end, upon the throne of David, and upon His kingdom, to order it, and to establish it with judgment and with justice from henceforth even forever. The zeal of the Lord of hosts will perform this"* (*Isaiah 9:6-7*). There has never been a government like the one soon to appear on planet Earth. It will be perfect, in every way. God is most determined to bring it, and the last phrase of this passage proves it.

A Government Without Flaws

When fully implemented, the government of God will be a picture of harmony and unity, with all those in administration being the right choice for each job, perfectly qualified for the tasks they face.

We have seen that Christ rules with the saints, he will not use human beings to administer any government offices. But certain officials will need to be appointed. For instance, there may need to be police to help with community service and guidance. Notice this prophecy of Christ in Isaiah. It demonstrates His ability to pick the right officials for the right positions, based on character and what is in their heart: *"And the spirit of the Lord shall rest upon Him, the spirit of wisdom and understanding, the spirit of counsel and might, the spirit of knowledge and of the fear of the Lord; And shall make Him of quick understanding in the fear of the Lord: and He shall not judge after the sight of His eyes, neither reprove after the hearing of His ears: But with righteousness shall He judge the poor, and reprove with equity for the meek of the earth: and He shall smite the earth with the rod of His mouth, and with the breath of His lips shall He slay the wicked"* (Isaiah 11:2-4).

This is a marvelous, wonderful prophecy of how Christ will rule in perfect righteousness. He will crush all opposition to His rule. He will not play favorites, using nepotism or cronyism. Christ will not take bribes or kickbacks for granting unfair advantage to those with money or influence. Imagine no more competing political parties currying favor and promoting division for political advantage in an election. All fighting, arguing and "deal-making" will come to an end. The saints, then born of God (*Romans 8:29; John 3:6; Colossians 1:18*), will be appointed over all governmental offices. Some will reign over ten cities, others five (*Luke 19:17-19*).

Christ's government will be a model of efficiency. It will be missing the botched, bungled, wasteful, red-tape-laden and painfully slow committee -driven decision-making of all man's forms of government. Gone will be officials who practice these things: *"None calls for justice, nor any pleads for truth: they trust in vanity, and speak lies; they conceive mischief, and bring forth iniquity...Their feet run to evil, and they make haste to shed innocent blood: their thoughts are thoughts of iniquity; wasting and destruction are in their paths. The way of peace they know not; and there is no judgment in their goings: they have made them crooked paths: whosoever goes therein shall not know peace"* (Isaiah 59:4, 7-8). Is this not exactly how city, state, provincial and federal governments work? Is this not what you hear people commonly express? Then they conclude, speaking of corrupt, *wrong* government: *"Therefore is judgment far from us, neither does justice overtake us: we wait for light, but behold obscurity; for brightness, but we walk in darkness. We grope for the wall like the blind, and we grope as if we had no eyes: we stumble at noonday as in the night; we are in desolate places as dead men..."* (*Isaiah 59:9-10*). *Verse 20* continues by explaining that *"the Redeemer [Christ] shall come to Zion,"* because this is humanity's only hope for solving such massive problems".

The next chapter is actually a continuation of what humanly-devised chapter and verse divisions tend to lose. It is what all mankind will be told: *"Arise, shine; for your light is come, and the glory of the Lord is risen upon you"* (*Isaiah 60:1*). All during my childhood, my mother awakened me each morning for school with the very same words "Arise [and] shine." Little did she know of the glorious event her daily announcement foretold.

Seven Millennial Days

Cut off from God by sin (*Isaiah 59:1-2*), mankind has believed the lies of the god of this world for 6,000 years. The core of God's Plan encompasses 7,000 years. Few know this. More have understood at least some verses describing Christ's 1,000-year reign, which will begin at the time of His Return to earth in great power and glory to rule with the saints (*Revelations 20:4-6*). While most know little more than this, they know nothing of the fact that God has allotted 6,000 years, or six millennial days of a *"seven-day week,"* to man's rule, prior to the seventh 1,000-year "day." The sixth "day" is about to draw to a close.

God is not losing a wrestling match with Satan for the salvation of the world. He knows exactly what He is doing, and His plan *can* be known. The true God would never condemn the vast millions without giving them a full opportunity for salvation. We must grasp what the Bible says: *"But, beloved, be not ignorant of this one thing, that one day is with the Lord as a thousand years, and a thousand years as one day"* (*II Peter 3:8*). Of course, most people *are* "ignorant" of not just this "one thing," but almost everything that the Bible teaches. This is a fascinating verse.

Man, under Satan's unseen influence, has been given six days, or 6,000 years, to try his own ways, governments, religions, philosophies, value systems and forms of education. He has practiced sin, disobedience to God's commands, for nearly 6,000 years, under the sway of Satan. He has then tried to treat all of the ill *effects* instead of treating the *cause* of having broken God's laws. These six 1,000-year "days of man" will soon be over. God is allowing man to learn bitter lessons. The masses, who have never known the precious truth of God, are having to learn that their ways do not work, but God's ways do.

Though heralded as "the world's last chance" The United Nations, like the League of Nations before it, has utterly failed in its purpose. Anyone who watches its actions understands that it is better described as "The Divided Nations. Now continue with *II Peter*. Notice *verse 9*: *"The Lord is not slack concerning His promise…but is longsuffering to us-ward, not willing that any should perish, but that all should come to repentance."* Did you notice that God wants to save *everyone*? When speaking of God (Christ) Paul states, *"Who will have all men to be saved, and to come unto the knowledge of the truth"* (*I Timothy 2:4*). The plain truth of this verse; God is not, and never has been, in the "mass condemnation" business.

As the master deceiver Satan has proliferated many forms of false religion and has hidden God's Plan from the nations. But, there is coming a 1,000-year "Sabbath rest." The seventh-day Sabbath was hallowed by God at creation in *Genesis 2:1-2*. Mankind will rest from sin and from the relentless deceit of the devil. Satan's time will soon be up, he is angrier now than ever before. *Mark 2:28* states, *"…the Son of man is Lord also of the sabbath."* Satan would have to be bound during this millennial Sabbath. It is vitally important to understand this tremendous truth. Satan's dominion will come to an end and the entire world will rest from sin when Christ comes as King of kings and Lord of lords. Christ's Return will be further examined later.

Soon the whole world will see the fulfillment of *Revelation 11:15*: *"The kingdoms of this world are become the kingdoms of our Lord, and of His Christ; and He shall reign forever and ever."* Just as there is no doubt that countries today represent real, literal, physical kingdoms (governments), there can be no doubt, from this verse, that God's coming government is also real and literal. Jesus Christ was born to be a King who will rule all nations, assisted by other spirit-composed kings: *"And out of His mouth goes a sharp sword, that with it He should smite the nations: and He shall rule them with a rod of iron…and on His thigh a name written, King of kings, and Lord of lords"* (*Revelations 19:15-16*). Has anyone ever told you of these verses? I never learned or even heard of them in the church of my youth, and yet, here they are, written with unmistakable clarity of meaning.

Understanding the New Covenant

Many are confused about the New Covenant. They suppose it to be little more than that would-be Christians are to "give their hearts to Jesus" or "accept the Lord" and they can be pronounced "saved." The teaching generally follows that God's Law has been "done away" and that "Jesus kept it for us." But is this really the New Covenant, the presumed purpose of the New Testament?

As a matter of fact, it is the opposite of what the Bible teaches. Notice: *"For this is the covenant that I will make with the house of Israel after those days, says the Lord; I will put My laws into their mind, and write them in their hearts: and I will be to them a God, and they shall be to Me a people"* (*Hebrews 8:10*). This is plain! The New Covenant has to do with people obeying God, and when God's government is established around the earth, this means everyone.

Here is how it will happen: *"But in the last days it shall come to pass, that the mountain of the house of the Lord shall be established in the top of the mountains, and it shall be exalted above the hills; and people shall flow unto it. And many nations shall come, and say, Come, and let us go up to the mountain of the Lord, and to the house of the God of Jacob; and He will teach us of His ways, and we will walk in His paths: for the law shall go forth of Zion, and the word of the Lord from Jerusalem. And He shall judge among many people, and rebuke strong nations afar off; and they shall beat their swords into plowshares, and their spears into pruning hooks: nation shall not lift up a sword against nation, neither shall they learn war any more"* (*Micah 4:1-3*).

In front of the United Nations Building is the sculptured image of a large man forging a plow from a sword, I have seen it many times. Soon this depiction will be reality. The world will initially resist such radical change. They will prefer the over 30 million laws of men, which are so contradictory and unjustly enforced. They will have to learn that *"There is a way that seems right unto a man, but the end thereof are the ways of death"* (*Proverbs 14:12; 16:25*). Men will learn that they have not known real right from real wrong!

The whole world will learn why God told ancient Israel, through Moses, *"You shall not do after all the things that we do here this day, every man whatsoever is right in his own eyes...Take heed to yourself that you be not snared by following them, after that they be destroyed from before*

you; and that you inquire not after their gods, saying, How did these na-
tions serve their gods? Even so will I do likewise. You shall not do so
unto the Lord your God: for every abomination to the Lord, which He
hates, have they done unto their gods…" (Deuteronomy 12:8, 30-31).

When men follow their own feelings and dictates, they get into trouble. Civilization is a testimony to how many "gods," and how many pagan customs and practices, people can dream up and follow. After doing this for a few generations, such "gods" and practices "seem right." They feel good and become comfortable. But men's opinions do not make them good. When Christ enacts His Plan to re-educate and spiritually convert all nations, He will crush all rebellion against His ways and all wrong religious and social customs by supernatural force. Every one of God's laws will be, quite literally, religiously enforced. There will be no exceptions!

This will mean the complete disappearance of all forms of disobedience. In light of the rampant fear of crime and violence that exists today, what an incredible utopian atmosphere just this change will make.

God's Holy Days to be Universally Observed

Following pagan customs for thousands of years, the world's religions have practiced pagan holidays condemned in the Bible, counterfeit Christianity having been the worst! Christmas, Easter, Halloween, New Year's, Valentine's Day and others have never had anything to do with the true God. These are all man-made customs that have been "Christianized" by a rebellious, counterfeit Christianity, seeking to legitimize what God has outlawed. These and the rest of the world's *substitute,* supposedly "Christian", customs will disappear forever with the augmentation of Christ's rule. In their place will be kept God's seven annual festivals. Mankind will be required to observe these wonderful feasts, which are full of real meaning, revealing what has always been God's purpose. They picture the major events and lessons of His 7,000-year Plan, previously discussed.

God gave His Holy Days to ancient Israel, and she rejected and replaced them with counterfeits. Yet Christ and the apostles kept them. As did the early New Testament Church (*John 7:2, 37; Acts 18:21; 20:6; I Cor. 5:7 -8; 16:8*). This included all Gentile converts. Man's holidays are kept according to his choice of seasons. In the world tomorrow, God's annual festivals will be kept in *their* appointed seasons around the world: *"And it shall come to pass, that every one that is left of all the nations [those not supernaturally destroyed in the war of Zechariah 14:12] which came against Jerusalem shall even go up from year to year to worship the King, the Lord of hosts, and to keep the feast of tabernacles" (Zechariah. 14:16).*

Some nations will resist and refuse to obey. However, none will be permitted to remain exceptions. Christ will have to use His "rod of iron" on some countries to bring universal obedience to these special days: *"And it shall be, that whoso will not come up of all the families [nations] of the earth unto Jerusalem to worship the King, the Lord of Hosts, even upon them shall be no rain. And if the family of Egypt go not up, and come not, that have no rain; there shall be the plague, wherewith the Lord will smite the heathen that come not up to keep the feast of tabernacles. This shall be the punishment of Egypt, and the punishment of all nations that come not up to keep the feast of tabernacles" (Zechariah 14:17-19).*

God is serious about obedience. No longer will false ministers deceive millions into believing that the Holy Days were "done away" or were "part of Moses' law" or only "for the Jews." There were twelve Israelite tribes, with the Jews being only one. *God's* Holy Days were for much more than just "the Jews." Egypt is a Gentile nation. This passage reveals that all non-Israelite nations must comply with God's festivals. And, by keeping them, all peoples will remain mindful of the Master Plan that God is working out. The world will come to understand the wonderful blessing of keeping God's days. But it will take God's all-powerful government to insure that this happens.

Preparation and Training of Ruling Team Begun Long Ago

God has not been idle during the thousands of years of man's rule. He has used this time to prepare those who will lead with Christ when His government is restored on the earth. Many important positions must be filled by those qualified and trained for appointment to high office. Once again, God will not hand great power and authority to any who have not been specifically trained, or carefully prepared, in how to use it. Even newly-elected human governments are given at least some time to interview various candidates and nominees for important jobs, before making critical appointments. Qualifications are carefully considered, usually by several people, before announcing appointees. Would God not do the same? And, since He has had from the time of creation to plan, would He not have carefully called, trained and prepared certain ones for very specific roles before making His selection? Of course! God will not select or use selfish politicians only interested in fulfilling personal ambition, based on their ability to "politic" their way into His kingdom. Nor will He reward those who are simply most skilled at surviving the typical "palace intrigue" of this world's governments. We have seen that His Plan is far more equitable, just, and much bigger in long-term planning and preparation than any government of man.

In the next section we will examine certain familiar Bible figures and see how their training in this life has prepared them for specific positions of service for all eternity within God's kingdom. All aspects of government; economy, education and religion, have been pre-planned for by God. He will soon be ready to unveil an entire spiritual "cabinet" to surround Christ, comprised of the most highly qualified leaders the world, and the universe, have ever seen!

Abraham, Isaac and Jacob

It will be evident that God has prepared numerous leaders in special ways so that their talents and qualifications will enhance His perfect government. In several places, the Bible speaks of the unique relationship between Abraham, Isaac and Jacob. As grandfather, father and son, they are prophesied to be among God's greatest leaders, and will no doubt serve as a team in the kingdom of God. They are often referred to in scripture as "The Fathers." Few others are mentioned specifically regarding salvation. Notice: *"There shall be weeping and gnashing of teeth, when you shall see Abraham, and Isaac, and Jacob, and all the prophets, in the kingdom of God, and you yourselves thrust out" (Luke 13:28).*

The most prominent and faithful person in God's "pre-training" program is Abraham. The book of Genesis reveals him as a man of exemplary character and integrity. When God told Abraham, originally Abram, to *"Get you out of your country, and from your kindred, and from your father's house, unto a land that I will show you" (Genesis 12:1),* God records, *"So Abram departed" (Genesis 12:4).* Without argument or excuse-making, Abraham took his servants and left *all* that was familiar to him. How many people would do this? Later in Genesis, God records more about Abraham's complete faithfulness to *every* instruction God gave him: *"Because that Abraham obeyed My voice, and kept My charge, My commandments, My statutes, and My laws" (Genesis 26:5).*

In *Galatians 3:29, Gentiles* there were told, *"And if you be Christ's, then are you Abraham's seed [children], and heirs according to the promise." Verse 7* states that all those of faith are *"children of Abraham." Verse 16* states that to Abraham and *his* children *"were the promises made."* This is a key understanding. Obviously, Abraham stands above all those whom God considers to be His children. Because of his obedience and behavior during certain extremely difficult trials and tests, God gave Abraham enormous blessings, including great wealth and personal possessions. He also had 318 trained servants at his disposal, this gave him experience in managing large resources and numbers of people. This obedient and faithful man trained his son Isaac to be the same. Isaac became an heir with Abraham, and Old Testament accounts show that he was obedient and extremely faithful to instructions given him.

Abraham's grandson Jacob also gained tremendous personal wealth. As a result of trials with his father-in-law, he learned important lessons of faithfulness, honor and follow-through. He was a never-give-up person of extraordinary leadership. The Bible states that he *"prevailed"* with God (*Genesis 32:28*). And, of course, he had thirteen children, twelve sons and one daughter, which gave him valuable management experience. His parental guidance must have been quite exceptional, because prophecy shows that his twelve sons fathered perhaps the twelve greatest nations of the world tomorrow. We will see later that Joseph, Jacob's second youngest son, was uniquely trained for his position.

Organizational Pattern Revealed

Let's fill in some more key positions in God's overall governmental structure. God does not tell us in exact detail every capacity in which each leader will serve. But the Bible does offer clues, if we search for them. Some are more direct than others.

Of course, God the Father is Supreme Authority over all matters in the universe. Christ is number two as King of kings and Lord of lords. He is the Father's executive administrator over all things. Christ acknowledged, *"My Father is greater than I"* (*John 14:28*). As awesome as is Christ's power and authority, He fully understands His role as second-in-command. He will not, like Satan, ever be tempted to try to overthrow God. Neither will any others who serve under Him. They will have *proven* their loyalty to God's government during their human lifetimes. Under Christ, David will be over all of the twelve tribes of Israel. Christ stated that the twelve apostles would be over each of the twelve tribes, after they are physically re-composed as nations at the outset of the millennium.

From this basic understanding comes the overall organizational pattern of government from which we can deduce certain other likely appointees within it.

Church and State Will Work Together

Several modern democracies practice what is commonly referred to as "the separation of church and state." The United States attempts to observe this most stringently, while at the same time asserting "In God We Trust." This kind of thinking springs from the idea that *civil* authority should be distinctly separate from & unrelated to *religious* authority. While this is certainly better if that civil authority is in the hands of carnal human beings, it is not the way it should be. Nor is it the way things will be under God's perfect government.

In tomorrow's world Church and State *will* work together, in harmony, without endless legal challenges designed to test the limits of where government should or should not intrude into religion. Neither will religion need to be restrained from involving itself in government. These restraints and limitations are all artificial and humanly-devised. They are based on the idea that God should be *excluded* from all matters of government. This will be unthinkable when God is in authority.

The very gospel message that Jesus Christ brought is almost entirely about government. Men have never wanted God's, or any other, government over them. Most have no idea that the Bible is primarily a book about government, why men's governments never work, and why God's pattern is the only one that does. In a world where men do not trust one another, and often cannot agree on even the most basic principles and judgments, they want separation, with no one able to *interfere* with their power base and decision-making. Competition is practiced instead of *cooperation* because men cannot see that cooperation multiplies and competition divides. There will be absolute unity in every aspect of God's government, and it will not be based on compromise. All leaders, at every level, will seek and find agreement, because all will be in agreement with Christ, who agrees with God. Government, education, religion and social functions will all be unified, because everyone will be working toward the same end.

The Bible offers important clues about which men, when resurrected as divine spirit-beings, will work together over matters of Church and State. *Matthew 17:1-9* describes Peter, James and John seeing a vision of the kingdom of God. They saw Christ, with Moses and Elijah, together in full glory. Take a moment to read it and consider the lives of these two towering Bible figures. *After six days Jesus took with him Peter, James and John the brother of James, and led them up a high mountain by themselves. There he was transfigured before them. His face shone like the sun, and his clothes became as white as the light. Just then there appeared before them Moses and Elijah, talking with Jesus. Peter said to Jesus, "Lord, it is good for us to be here. If you wish, I will put up three shelters - one for you, one for Moses and one for Elijah." While he was still speaking, a bright cloud covered them, and a voice from the cloud said, "This is my Son, whom I love; with him I am well pleased. Listen to him!" When the disciples heard this, they fell facedown to the ground, terrified. But Jesus came and touched them. "Get up," he said. "Don't be afraid." When they looked up, they saw no one except Jesus. As they were coming down the mountain, Jesus instructed them, "Don't tell anyone what you have seen, until the Son of Man has been raised from the dead."*

Consider first Moses who spent 40 years administrating, with absolute civil authority, over the millions of Israelites whom God delivered from Egypt. This gave him extensive experience in matters of judgment, leadership and decision-making. He learned, sometimes from trial and error, how to appoint judges and princes over the masses of Israel he brought from Sinai and administered God's law over ancient Israel. God used him to record the five books of the Law, called the Pentateuch, that are the first five books of the Bible. His training in Egypt, as a member of Pharaoh's royal family until age 40, established a foundation of practical experience that God used after his conversion in the land of Midian. His training involved 40 years of living and working with Gentiles and 40 years as leader of the children of Israel. This background would seem to make him uniquely qualified to administer all matters of state, national and international, under the government of God.

Now consider Elijah. This Old Testament prophet was so exemplary in service that God typed him through two of His greatest servants, foretold to come later, who were also called "Elijahs" (*Malachi 4:5-6; Matthew 17:11-13*). Much space is devoted to Elijah in the books of First and Second Kings. He led and inspired an unparalleled restoration of observing

God's Ten Commandments and the worship of the true God, after Israel had fallen into Baal and Astaroth worship (*I Kings 18:19-39*). This account culminates in *verse 39* with the people, after witnessing Elijah's miracle, confessing, *"The Lord [Eternal], He is the God; the Lord [Eternal], He is the God."*

Elijah also organized and led three colleges or schools at Jericho, Gilgal and Bethel, for the purpose of instructing in God's Law and truth in the midst of a world filled with false pagan education and religion (*II Kings 2:3 & 5; 4:38*). Understand that, perhaps more than anything else, Elijah was a religious educator. This man was essentially responsible for all "church activity" in Israel. His training has made him eminently qualified to serve beside Moses, as they together head up Church and State!

Israel Under God's Government

Now let's examine more about what numerous prophecies reveal to be the greatest nations of the world tomorrow, the twelve tribes of Israel. They offer greater insight into God's pattern of organization within His government.

Recall that David will be appointed over Israel's twelve tribes. God is most plain about this role. Speaking of Israel in the millennium, *Jeremiah 30:9* states, *"But they shall serve the Lord their God, and David their king, whom I will raise up unto them."* Ezekiel adds more about David's appointment in two places: *"And I will set up one shepherd over them, and he shall feed them, even My servant David; he shall feed them, and he shall be their shepherd. And I the Lord will be their God, and My servant David a prince among them (Ezekiel 37:24-25);* *"I the Lord have spoken it"* (*Ezekiel 34:23-24*). It would seem certain that David will serve under Moses over the tribes of Israel.

Christ told His twelve apostles that they would each lead one of the twelve tribes of Israel in the "regeneration", the resurrection: *"And Jesus said unto them, Verily I say unto you, that you which have followed Me, in the regeneration when the Son of man shall sit in the throne of His glory, you also shall sit upon twelve thrones, judging the twelve tribes of Israel"* (*Matthew 19:28*). Understand this critical point that has become lost to the world, the Jews are only <u>one twelfth</u> of the tribes of Israel! They sprang from Jacob's son Judah. There were eleven *other* sons. All but two grew into modern nations present on earth today, the children of Simeon and Levi are scattered. From one son, Joseph, a great nation and a company of nations sprang. Out of his sons, Ephraim and Manasseh, came modern Britain and the United States. Prophecy shows that these are again to be the two single greatest nations on earth in the world tomorrow (*Jeremiah 30:16-18; 31:4-11, 18-20; Isaiah 14:1-2; Deuteronomy 28:13*). The other tribes of Israel will be next to them, with God's blessings also then poured out on all Gentile nations.

There will be many other rulers over portions of the twelve tribes of Israel. Whether rulers serve as mayors, governors or kings, they will all be composed of spirit, resurrected members of the ruling God Family. Their selection will reflect a lifetime of growing, overcoming and qualifying in matters of God's government, leadership and law.

Overcomers Qualify

An important inset is necessary here, the book of Revelation contains three powerful verses showing that Christians are called to qualify for future rulership. Christ instructs us, *"And he that overcomes, and keeps My works unto the end, to him will I give power over the nations: And he shall rule them with a rod of iron..."* (*Revelations 2:26-27*). Now notice this verse: *"To him that overcomes will I grant to sit with Me in My throne, even as I also overcame, and am set down with My Father in His throne"* (*Revelations 3:21*). These verses also describe the re-establishing of God's government over all nations. Christians who overcome will receive power to rule. One more verse in Revelation summarizes the previous two: *"And has made us unto our God kings and priests: and we shall reign on the earth"* (*Revelations 5:10*). Kings and priests are teachers; all those called of God are in training to instruct others. This is why Christ's New Testament commission to His Church is, *"Go you therefore, and teach all nations"* (*Matthew 28:19*). His Church is learning to teach now.

Only a handful of people were called in the Old Testament, with just three, Abel, Enoch and Noah, called prior to the Flood. There may have been up to five more. After the Flood came the patriarchs and the prophets, with King David and a few others. God used most of these men for a special purpose or commission. But all were *trained* and had to *overcome* Satan, the temptations of his world and the pulls of the flesh. Christians overcome their problems, weaknesses, sins, wrong attitudes, and Satan's nature. Christ said, *"In the world you shall have tribulation: but be of good cheer; I have overcome the world"* (*John 16:33*). Christ had overcome both the world and its god. He said, *"even as I also overcame, and am set down with My Father in His throne."* By overcoming, Christ qualified to rule. Just as He qualified to replace Satan, so we too must qualify.

Such enormous power to rule could never be given to people who are un-prepared, who have not qualified to properly use it. God is not about *to* hand great authority to those who might rebel and revert to the ways of Satan. He cannot ever again have another "Lucifer-turned-Satan" cause destruction and chaos. It will be impossible for any in the ruling kingdom of God to sin (*I John 3:9*). All people whom God calls will be judged ac-cording to how they developed their individual character What each ac-complished, with the talents he was given from birth, in the amount of time allotted to him. Both the parable of the talents (*Matthew 25:14-30*) and the pounds (Luke 19:11-27) reveal that Christians are qualifying for rulership over individual cities; some five cities, others ten cities, etc.

In the Parable of the Pounds Christ *"called"* His *"ten servants"*, as Christians being called out of this world by God, and instructed them to increase the worth of a pound (money) that He gave to each of them for investment. He told them to *"Occupy till I come"* or to *"grow"* the pound into more money. They understood that the Nobleman of the par-able (Christ) was coming to "reign" on earth. Upon the Nobleman's re-turn, He called each servant into His presence for a report of how each man had increased the pound that he had been given. Some had gained five pounds, others ten, etc., but one servant buried his pound in the ground and produced nothing with it. Christ wanted an accounting of how *"each man had gained"* while He had been away. The first servant had gained *ten* pounds and Christ explained his reward by saying, *"you good servant: because you have been faithful in a very little, have you authority over ten cities"* (*vs. 17*). The servant who had gained *five* pounds was put *"over five cities."* Because the second servant produced half as much, his reward was half as great. So, these men were given "authority", they were put into positions of rulership "over cities." Their reward was to "reign" with Christ (*Jude 14*) in His world-ruling king-dom. How obvious the purpose of our calling.

When the Parable of the Pounds speaks of some of the Noblemen's citi-zens *"hating Him,"* and states that they said, *"We will not have this Man to reign over us,"* it shows that some do not want the true Christ telling them what to do. They do *not* want Him to rule over their lives and con-duct. They certainly *do* want salvation, but with no strings attached. No one will receive rulership before proving that he *can be ruled.* No one can rule in God's perfect *ruling government* unless he has learned to *sub-*

mit to that government and be ruled by God in *this* life. This is the first all-important lesson of the Parable of the Pounds.

Also, when Christ called His servants into account, He was showing that all people will one day stand and give account before the judgment seat of Christ. Like the reward of the twelve apostles (*Matthew 19:27-28*), some will be given great authority to rule over cities with Christ. This is the second vital lesson of the parable.

Gentile Oversight

We next come to those most likely to hold key positions of rulership over the Gentile nations. The prophet Daniel gained much experience, in his direct relationship as number three in authority (Daniel 5:7) under perhaps the greatest Gentile king of all time, Babylonian King Nebuchadnezzar.

Though completely pagan, both in customs and worship of false gods, Babylon is described as possibly the greatest Gentile empire the world has seen. This alone makes Daniel's experience unique. Yet, when under immense pressure to compromise, he proved himself utterly loyal to the true God and His ways. He sought God three times daily. God even used Daniel to record the promise of his own resurrection (*Daniel 12:13*). Daniel did not compromise any of God's ways or laws, even when threatened with death in a lion's den.

Ezekiel 14:14 & 20 describes *"Noah, Daniel and Job"* as three of the most righteous men of all time (we will examine Noah and Job momentarily). This, coupled with Daniel's particular circumstances, strongly suggests that his wisdom and knowledge in matters of national and international government qualify him for the highest office, under Moses, over Gentiles. He demonstrated exceptional understanding in delicate matters of state and in his dealings with corrupt politicians surrounding Nebuchadnezzar. Think about how many governors, rulers and kings Daniel would have been familiar with in the day-to-day affairs of government. Could it be that Shadrach, Meshach and Abednego will serve as the top three assistants on his team?

Some might suppose that Paul, as the apostle to the Gentiles, is a more natural choice than any other to administer over the Gentiles. Certainly his experience was extraordinary, but not of the same type or scope as Daniel. But what is Paul's probable position of rulership in the government of God? Bear this in mind. Paul was the apostle to all Gentile areas. This represented far more authority and experience than any of the original twelve apostles held or received. Yet they are to rule the tribes of Israel, which will be greatest in size during Christ's millennial rule. It would seem virtually impossible that Paul would just be over any one Gentile country, no matter how large. The indication is that he will probably assist Daniel over all Gentile nations. The experiences of Timothy, Titus, Luke, Mark, Barnabas, Silas, Philemon and others, with Paul, indicate that they will probably work directly with Paul in certain key positions over regions, districts or groupings of cities in the possible role of governorships.

International Administration

International relations is sorely lacking in this world. There is much "diplomacy" but to very little good effect. Of course, the world's problems defy even the best work of modern, so-called diplomats. Teaching nations to work in harmony with one another, instead of in constant competition and strife, will be critical to world peace. While no one person will do everything, there is one man whose training and background best qualifies him to work on the international level in this way.

Noah lived the first two-thirds of his life in a world rife with problems between races. Seeing interracial marriage, racial violence and hatred, as well as previously mentioned corruption, violence and chaos on a worldwide scale, places Noah's experience at the top of those qualified to understand the cause and effect of how God's laws work toward international peace and harmony. God intended that peoples live within specific boundaries (*Deuteronomy 32:8-9; Acts 17:26*). He intended that they work together, cooperate in all important matters. He did not intend for them to amalgamate into one giant "world nation," as was happening prior to the Flood. Noah was used by God to warn the world for 120 years, explaining why crime, violence and corruption were exploding among all civilization. He witnessed, firsthand, why peoples could not get along. He lived through a "population explosion" *Genesis 6:1*, and saw its correlation to all problems between races;crime, riots, hatred, war and its direct relationship to the worst social troubles that plague civilizations.

It seems almost certain that Noah will be responsible for worldwide relocation of peoples, refugees, freed captives, illegal immigrants, colonial descendants, etc. to the places that God selects. Obviously, this will be an enormous task. It will not happen overnight. Massive food, lodging and transportation concerns will have to be addressed just in the initial relocation. Once again, nations and kindred will be forced to live where *God* chooses, and always intended. Of course, the entire world will have to go through a very difficult humbling process before this can happen (*Isaiah 2:10-12, 17*). But resistance will be suppressed, and humanity will love the end result.

Reconstruction and Food Procurement

While Noah is well qualified for this gigantic task, he will need high-ranking assistants to address the needs of people of all nations. God has prepared two men who would seem to be uniquely qualified to assist Noah.

Civilization will soon enter a time of terrible calamity on a global scale. It is prophesied that the devastation of past wars will be pale compared to what is coming. Whole nations and cities will be destroyed on a scale never seen before. This means reconstruction and rebuilding projects on a scale never seen before. Notice this prophecy in Isaiah: *"And they shall build the old wastes, they shall raise up the former desolations, and they shall repair the waste cities, the desolations of many generations"* (*Isaiah 61:4*). Mankind has generally been in the *de*-struction business. But God has always been in the *con*-struction business. As cities, towns and villages are rebuilt, they will be made beautiful everywhere, reflecting worldwide prosperity. Urban blight and slums will become things of the past. Spacious, attractive parks will be plentiful. City planners of the future will always be certain to allow enough room for people to enjoy their homes and the land around them. But the planning of this world's cities has been much different. Overpopulation has translated into over-crowding, with tenement houses teeming with too many people for the space allotted. Row houses are common in many big cities of the world. God says, *"Woe unto them that join house to house, that lay field to field, till there be no place..."* (*Isaiah 5:8*). Many of today's cities are better off temporarily becoming waste places. It will be far easier to rebuild them from scratch. Obeying God's laws of agriculture will result in a great abundance and high quality of grains, livestock, fruits and vegetables. The cities of the world to come will present a far different, and infinitely better and more beautiful, picture than the cities of today.

But who is most naturally qualified to assist Noah and head up such nation re-building? The Bible records that Job was one of the wealthiest and greatest men of his time (*Job 1:3*). Apparently, among his business ventures, he was very successful in construction (*Job 3:13-14; 38:4-6*). The entire book of Job describes a man of incredible temperance, self-control. God had to teach him humility and bring him to repentance through a series of most difficult trials. Job had to learn to rely completely on God, as a result of tests that were probably beyond what any single human being has had to endure. But his skill in building and developing, as evidenced by his vast holdings described in the Bible, would seem to qualify him to direct the enormously challenging and difficult task of, quite literally, re-developing the entire surface of the earth. The reconstruction of national infrastructures, bridges, roads, water purification, sewer systems, power plants, sanitation management, etc, will be sufficient to stagger thousands of civil engineers. Job, possibly assisted by Zerubbabel (*Haggai 2:23; Zechariah 4*), will be up to the task of re-building a magnificent, dazzling super civilization.

In light of the above-mentioned prophesied devastation to earth's surface, food and water shortages will also exist on a global scale. Someone will have to be certain that the starving masses have something to eat at the outset of Christ's 1,000-year rule be able to *expand* food production for a growing re-population of the earth. There is a man seemingly perfectly trained for this task. We will see that Joseph is the logical choice. First, recall that he is the father of Ephraim and Manasseh, who are prophesied to be the two greatest nations in the new world. Joseph and his sons (and the countries that sprang from them) have the greatest experience in global economics of any men or nations of the past. Genesis records this of Joseph, after he was humbled through very difficult and trying circumstances: *"And the Lord was with Joseph, and he was a prosperous man; and he was in the house of his master the Egyptian. And his master saw that the Lord was with him, and that the Lord made all that he did to prosper in his hand"* (*Genesis 39:2-3*).

The Bible records that Egypt, the greatest nation of its day, endured a seven-year famine on the heels of seven years of plenty. Joseph engineered and managed the extra storage, and later distribution, of vast food reserves that saw Egypt through this long famine. Just the administration and duration of this single task required extraordinary skill, planning, delegation and ingenuity. Who, throughout history, has ever navigated a great nation through such extensive famine? It appears obvious that Joseph will be the director of collective commerce, industry, agriculture, technology, banking, etc. He will probably be in charge, on an international scale, of the entire new economy, and will be responsible for eradicating all poverty and famine, working alongside Job to provide food and shelter to a shattered humanity.

But there are other supremely important matters of administration in tomorrow's wonderful world!

Chapter IV: One World Religion & Universal Education

The devil *"deceives the whole world" (Revelations 12:)*. By now, you realize that this deception will come to an end. His cunning and deceptive reasoning will be gone, but it must be replaced by *right* thinking. God's Word is plain regarding His final solution to Satan's global seduction!

There are many wonderful prophecies describing the marvelous utopia of tomorrow's world. But few are as all-encompassing in impact as this prophecy in Isaiah: *"They shall not hurt nor destroy in all My holy mountain: for the earth shall be full of the knowledge of the Lord, as the waters cover the sea" (Isaiah 11:)*. Grasp this powerful verse. It pictures a marvelous time that is almost beyond comprehension. Stop and think. The only religious knowledge then available to humanity will be what *God* teaches. Christ and the saints will teach *this* knowledge, as Christ's feet stand on the Mount of Olives (*Zechariah 14:*), and His throne is established, He says, *"My reward is with Me, to give every man according as his work shall be" (Revelations 22:1)*. This is when all those who are *"heirs"* with Christ (*Romans 8:1*) shall *"inherit the kingdom"* (*Matthew 25:3*). *Matthew 2* describes the parable of the *"sheep and goats."* It depicts *"all nations"* sitting before Christ on His *"throne of glory"* separating His sheep (true Christians) from all those who reject God's way.

At this time, all positions of rulership (reward) are given to the resurrected, immortal saints. Their first task is to spread God's truth around the world in the greatest evangelistic crusade of spiritual re-education ever. This will have to include the enormous task of helping up to one-half of humanity overcome illiteracy, and learn to read and write. Short of this, it will be impossible for people to learn God's ways. The next two verses in *Isaiah 1* show that all Gentiles will seek Christ after He gathers the peoples of Israel back to their own land. *Romans 11:25-2* describes God's Plan to include and convert Gentiles: *"For I would not, brethren, that you should be ignorant...that blindness in part is happened to Israel, until the fullness of the Gentiles be come in. And so all Israel shall be saved: as it is written, There shall come out of Zion the Deliverer, and shall turn away ungodliness from Jacob."*

Worldwide Education and Re-education

God can only work with people who can read the Bible. Salvation is absolutely impossible if people cannot read about the true God and His requirements and commands. *Basic* education, then, becomes absolutely essential for approximately one-half of the peoples on earth to even have an opportunity to be saved. The other half of mankind has been "educated", this means that they have been steeped in the world's false values, pagan religions & customs, the atheistic concept of evolution, and all the ways of Satan's nature instilled into people as human nature. This half has much to *unlearn*. They will not have to receive basic education as much as they will have to be *re-educated*. People will learn that much of the knowledge they swallowed as fact was little more than false indoctrination and propaganda, given them by the god of this world (*II Corinthians 4:*).

Humanity will have to learn that there is right knowledge and there is wrong knowledge, and how to know the difference. People will also learn the difference between spiritual and physical knowledge. It will be universally taught that the Bible is the foundation of all knowledge. Satan is the true father of this world's education. At that time, men will learn that they can no longer eat of the *"tree of the knowledge of good and evil,"* which is rooted in his thinking. All true knowledge comes from God, and mankind will understand that peace, happiness, abundance, universal health and prosperity spring from divine revelation. The fable that mankind is continually evolving into a "higher order" will be debunked and replaced with the knowledge that for 6,000 years man continually became more degenerate, decadent and depraved in conduct and thought.

Life is a process of education, learning to develop character by obedience to God's laws, which in turn yields every good, fulfilling and favorable result. Education in the world of tomorrow will explain how to live, and how to learn a productive trade. Of course, all academic subjects, including wholesome art and music, will produce well-rounded people. Life will become invigorating, exciting and fulfilling. Imagine how important world history will be in the classrooms of tomorrow. Everyone will be forced to view the truth of history through the eyes of God, instead of through the revisionist propaganda of each nation's historians; including their dishonest version of world history, written according to how they need to portray it. No one will be allowed to forget how, and how long, the world was off track from God's laws and ways. All error will be exposed for what it is. The truth of every matter, in every field of knowledge, will be taught in place of error. This will not be easy to do with everyone. Many will have been steeped in the false knowledge of this world's values, these will be deeply ingrained. Man-made definitions of political correctness, situation ethics, human rights, discrimination, alternative lifestyles and proper education will have to be scrapped and replaced with God's definitions. Some describe the Bible as "violent" or "hate literature." Many believe this, and they will have to unlearn it; forcibly if necessary.

The facts of *why* things happen a certain way will be taught in a straightforward fashion. No punches will be pulled. For instance, mankind will be taught exactly why war occurs, from God's perspective. Consider this from the book of James: *"From where come wars and fightings among you?" (James 4:).* The question is direct. So is God's answer: *"Come they not hence, even of your lusts that war in your members? You lust, and have not: you kill, and desire to have, and cannot obtain: you fight and war, yet you have not, because you ask not. You ask, and receive not, because you ask amiss, that you may consume it upon your lusts" (James 4:1-3). Verse* adds, *"Do you think that the scripture says in vain, The spirit that dwells in us lusts to envy?"* Plain, simple answers like these will be given in classrooms around the world. Gone will be vague, blurred, philosophical opinions; lacking the absolutes of God's Law and His explanations. But try to tell today's generals, soldiers and military planners such unvarnished truth about why they go to war and kill. They will ridicule your suggestion as so much unrealistic, childish idealism.

Re-educating the world will be a truly monumental task. The difficult job of teaching people to learn can only be done if teachers are *un*-handcuffed and allowed to bring proper discipline and order to schools and classrooms, now so out of control.

One Pure World Language Necessary

Perhaps the greatest single barrier to being sure all nations are taught the exact same thing, with no room for misunderstanding, are man's hundreds of different languages. All peoples must be given a pure language so that God's knowledge is not subject to the error of translators working in and out of hundreds of languages and dialects. The fulfillment of *Isaiah 11:* has to involve a simultaneous worldwide education program. In fact, the Bible directly prophesies the coming of this new, pure language to be spoken by all nations. Notice: *"For then will I turn to the people a pure language, that they may all call upon the name of the Lord, to serve Him with one consent" (Zephaniah 3:).*

Try to imagine a world with absolutely no communication barriers. It is a very different picture than today's world. Which begs the question why are there so many languages today? All during the pre-flood world, and for some time after, all peoples spoke a common language. *Genesis 11:* states, *"And the whole earth was of one language, and of one speech."* The world's first great arch-rebel, Nimrod, led an effort to build the Tower of Babel. His plan was to survive any future flood and defy God. Here is what happened: *"And the Lord said, Behold, the people is one, and they have all one language; and this they begin to do: and now nothing will be restrained from them, which they have imagined to do. Go to, let us go down, and there confound their language, that they may not understand one another's speech"* (*Genesis 11:6-*). God *"confounded their language"* and this barrier has remained. If God had not intervened, mankind would have realized technological breakthroughs, including lethal weapons of mass destruction, many centuries ago. Enormous evil would have resulted from the presence of one language, particularly with Satan still in power. Under his sway, nothing would have been restrained from a more unified mankind. Men would have committed world suicide long before the time of the end. God intervened to prevent such a catastrophe and to keep His Plan on a 6,000-year track.

In the new world, the need to slow the nations' progress toward calamity through different languages will no longer exist. Although the language barrier forestalled man's ability to annihilate himself, its continuation in tomorrow's world would be a stumbling block in understanding between nations, and would work against God's purpose. I have held many conversations, several lasting for hours, with people of other languages. When interpreters translate from one language to another, the subtleties of voice inflections, nuances of meaning, cultural dimensions (music, art, poetry, etc.) and other differences are lost.

People also use language to think. Generally, the language they speak directly affects, and even to some degree molds, their perspective on life; and causes their minds to work differently than others. In addition, Satan complicates the language barrier today by transmitting suspicion, hostility, and all the moods he broadcasts. When Satan is bound, and all the languages that have been slowly corrupted for millennia are replaced with a single pure language, all peoples will be much better able to serve God. The free exchange of ideas and cultural thought will dramatically improve. Imagine how many misunderstandings will never occur because everyone speaks words that carry universal meaning.

Languages Evolving or De-volving?

The history of language is fascinating, modern man thinks he has slowly evolved into a being of greater intelligence and understanding. He also believes that his languages have evolved from simple to complex, crude to sophisticated, and elementary to approaching perfection.

The facts reveal that, as man progresses, and his civilization becomes more "advanced," his language breaks down to a simpler state, with syntax and grammar rules compromised, violated or ignored. The less a society is exposed to the modern world and modern education, the better, and more pure, their languages remain. One prime example consists of the set of Chinese languages. Today these languages are primarily monosyllabic, with little or no grammatical guidelines. Linguists have discovered that this was not always the case. The further we look back in time, we find that the ancient Chinese language was far more complex than today, with predominantly polysyllabic word structures having stringent grammatical guidelines. A study of other languages reinforces this. Research at the Sorbonne at the University of Paris has confirmed that central African languages are not primitive by any standards, but are rather quite complex. They employ extensive abstract words, and nominal and verbal forms. The Bantu languages classify nouns into the categories of inanimate, animate, abstract, and so on. None of the more "advanced" languages use such precision. Swahili employs eight different noun classes. Latin or German makes the distinction between categories of gender (masculine, feminine, or neuter), while the nouns in Swahili are filtered and classified through eight different categories for more exact precision. Those who master such languages are seldom misunderstood. Some Bantu languages go well beyond the eight classes of Swahili and employ up to 26 noun classes, for even greater precision. The American Indians had languages with extensive vocabularies and grammatical structures that were systematic and very detailed. Some of the pronouns used by the Pacific Northwest tribes actually distinguish between the person near the speaker, near the person addressed, and of the person spoken of. Often the subject of the pronoun could even be classified as to whether or not it was visible. The more one studies language in our world, the more it becomes clear that the preserved ancient forms of languages are far superior to the broken down, eroded, streamlined and simplified modern languages. Therefore, it appears that the most developed nations actually employ languages that have the most degeneration and as languages progress alongside culture, they become less precise and less subject to systematic rules of grammar.

All modern languages have been corrupted. Many terms are borrowed from other languages. Languages also have many idioms that bear no resemblance to the actual words in an expression. This will all change soon. The pure language in tomorrow's world will certainly carry the precision of languages that have been preserved in their un-simplified forms. It will follow structured grammatical rules rather than the eroded, ambiguous languages that men have streamlined for convenience. Meaningless, ambiguous speech will become extinct. An entire generation of young people will have to learn how to speak properly. Many ancient cultures have written traditions of when the languages became divided. The basis of these traditions carries amazing resemblance, adding credence to what *Genesis* states. It is remarkable that those who devoutly hold to the "we are evolving upward" theory of evolution will not acknowledge such overwhelming evidence to the contrary.

Think about the tremendous expense that goes into the duplication of effort due to multitudes of different languages during this age. Much of this includes the reproduction of literature into different languages and the cost of translating and interpreting. Believe me, we know. The Work of God deals with this barrier daily. Imagine a world where everyone can communicate instantaneously with those of every other nationality.

Implementing One Language
Just as God instantaneously confounded the languages at Babel, He will suddenly implement the new universal language. There will not be the typical period of six months to two years for everyone to learn it. Perhaps some time may be necessary to refine writing skills and learn grammatical rules, but the ability of verbal communication will be immediate.

Only with one perfect language will every international barrier to peace truly disappear. In a world of seductive propaganda and *mis*-education, demagogues more easily gain control over people. Throughout history, when this happens, demagogues and foreign invaders usually executed both the nobility and the educated, because the illiterate masses more readily submit to dictatorships.

The plague of illiteracy will also vanish. Recognize that a leading cause of illiteracy is that great areas of the world do not even have language in written form. Among those that do, there are a variety of differing alphabets, such as Hebrew, Russian, Arabic, Greek and Sanskrit. Also gone will be the multiple ways that people pronounce the *same* words differently. Education and literacy will be universal in the world tomorrow, restoring dignity to all humanity, created in the image of God. All education will be administered or performed by the God Family, with everyone learning what God intends in the same way and at the same time, because all language confusion will be gone.

With proper education and no language barriers, *"the earth shall be full of the knowledge of the Lord, as the waters cover the sea"*.

A Capital City and Church

All governments have headquarters. The headquarters of the new world government will be Jerusalem (*Jeremiah. 3:1; Zechariah 14:*). While there may be government capitals of individual nations, they will all report directly to Jerusalem for direction in all governmental affairs, national and international.

From Jerusalem will come all spiritual instruction about God's Law, until every nation has been correctly indoctrinated with the new understanding of God's Law of love. A long passage in Isaiah explains how nations will look to Jerusalem for guidance and direction, and how they will be taught in matters of obedience to God: *"And it shall come to pass in the last days, that the mountain of the Lord's house shall be established in the top of the mountains, and shall be exalted above the hills; and all nations shall flow unto it. And many people shall go and say, Come you, and let us go up to the mountain of the Lord, to the house of the God of Jacob; and He will teach us of His ways, and we will walk in His paths: for out of Zion shall go forth the law, and the word of the Lord from Jerusalem. And He shall judge among the nations, and shall rebuke many people: and they shall beat their swords into plowshares, and their spears into pruninghooks: nation shall not lift up sword against nation, neither shall they learn war any more"* (*Isaiah 2:2-*). So that there is no misunderstanding how God intends His Law to blanket all nations, I have repeated this identical passage to the *Micah 4:1-* prophecy quoted earlier. These two passages speak of "mountains" and "hills." This is the Bible terminology for large nations and small nations. Therefore, peoples of *all* countries will be administered to by certain resurrected immortals that will be headquartered at Jerusalem. It will quickly be apparent around the world that God has chosen this city for His capital. Jerusalem literally means "city of peace", and all nations will be taught by those in the City of Peace not to *"learn war anymore."*

The first-century Church brought matters of doctrine and governmental administration to the apostles, who were headquartered at Jerusalem. *Acts 1* tells the story of a ministerial conference many attended to resolve questions within the Church. It reveals a pattern of how God's leading, highest-ranking ministers function from that city, from a headquarters. This conference produced final decisions, binding on the Church, and allowed right communication to answer questions and remove confusion. The early New Testament Church never used a doctrinal committee. Christ taught the Church directly through the apostles, Peter being leader among the twelve. As headquarters pastor, the apostle James issued decisions that God inspired. "Scholars" and "intellectuals," steeped in the false education of this world's institutions, will not be permitted to "voice their dissent" or submit papers for "doctrinal review and consideration." God's Church has always had a single leader. It is the job of this leader to adhere to the teachings of apostles, who are guided by Christ. There will be no deacon review boards, or other boards, to certify, hire or fire the leaders that God selects and installs for service where He wants them. God works from the top down, not the bottom up.

Abraham, Isaac, Jacob, Joseph, Noah, Daniel, Job, Moses and Elijah, among other top officials, will no doubt be headquartered in Jerusalem. There is some indication that Christians of the sixth era (Philadelphia) may serve in some direct capacity within the headquarters congregation of God's kingdom (*Revelations 3:1*). It also appears that John the Baptist, a type of Elijah (*Luke 1:1; Matthew 11:7-1; 17:10-1*), may work directly with or under Elijah. One that Christ would call *"the greatest born of women,"* would obviously have a very high office. It would seem that Elijah and John the Baptist will direct all education worldwide from the headquarters Church at Jerusalem. The dissemination of spiritual knowledge and doctrine will flow from headquarters as countries "flow" to Jerusalem for guidance. This means there will be vast numbers of individual Church congregations to be supervised. Their overall direction and administration around the world will come from headquarters, with various levels of administrative authority and responsibility by regional and area supervisors, pastors, elders, deacons, etc. Of course, as the Head of the Church (*Ephesians 1:2; 5:2; Colossians 1:1*), Christ will be the ultimate Director of Church Administration. All will be required to work in peace and harmony, to promote unity so that cooperation can replace the competition and division so prevalent in the churches of this world.

The ultimate task of headquarters will be to teach the vital spiritual knowledge necessary for salvation. Remember, it is at this time that God moves to save the masses. He has only been calling a relative few for the last 6,000 years. He will soon begin to work with millions. When it becomes His purpose to save the world, He will do it. All pastors will teach the way to happiness. They will teach the way of love; and how God's laws, His Commandments, have always been the path to real love between man and his neighbor, and between God and man (*Romans 13:1; I John 5:*). People will be taught to *"grow in grace and knowledge"* (*II Peter 3:1*) and to overcome pulls of the flesh and wrong impulses (*Revelations 3:1, 2*). They will be taught that Christianity is far more than a "decision for Jesus" and Satan's ministers (*II Corinthians 11:13-1*) will not be present to undermine and deceive about God's purposes.

How God Prepared Leaders

God began to work with and train most of His servants early in their adult lives. David was a young shepherd boy who had a wonderful attitude with which God could work (*I Samuel 16:6-, 11-1*). This allowed God to use him, after much training, as king over all Israel, instead of his seven older, apparently more physically impressive brothers. Moses was brought into Pharaoh's court as a baby, and trained for 80 years before assuming leadership of Israel. Joshua observed and assisted Moses for 40 years before replacing him at Moses' death. Paul was trained in the "back seat" for many years after conversion before God appointed him apostle to the Gentiles. Noah toiled in relative obscurity until age 480, before coming to prominence in warning the world. Even Christ was trained for 30 years before His ministry began.

Certainly God started with men of extraordinary ability, but all these men had many lessons to learn before they were prepared to assume great authority in this life. They had to learn to work with and manage people, to make difficult judgments, and to remain faithful and loyal to God and His laws, while enduring suffering and persecution. God made absolutely certain that all those who will serve in His coming, perfect government recognize that it is built on His perfect laws. How many have been trained in the seven laws of success? Most people have no idea how to *define* success, let alone how to *achieve* it, nor have they been taught the laws that govern it. Very few have been taught that such laws exist, yet they do! These laws, briefly explained, are:

- *First*, have the right goal - To be born into and rule in the kingdom of God.

- *Second*, obtain a right education - One with God's vital, essential, spiritual knowledge, while striving to *unlearn* the pagan, evolutionary, "me first," "get" way of thinking.
- *Third*, good health - Carefully build and maintain the physical body God has given you just as you build and maintain your spirit.
- *Fourth*, drive - Practice a way of life that moves you forward to every goal of value.
- *Fifth*, resourcefulness - Employ when facing difficult, complex matters or obstacles in order to learn to solve problems.
- *Sixth*, endurance - This is absolutely essential for a never-quit, never-give-up, always-press-on-to-victory approach to life (*Matthew 24:1; 10:2*).
- *Seventh*, reliance – Rely on God for guidance; through prayer, Bible study, meditation and periodic fasting. This is the single most indispensable quality for all leaders to maintain.

All God's servants generally knew and practiced these most basic laws. The entire 11th chapter of *Hebrews* is a fascinating study in the dedication, faith, courage, steadfastness, enduring spirit, vision, strength, determination, commitment and conviction of many of God's greatest leaders and pillars. It speaks of Enoch, Abel, Sarah, Gideon, Rahab, Barek, Samson, Jephthae and Samuel, among others. It tells of their enduring faith in God's purpose in their lives, and how they were qualifying for important roles in the kingdom of God. All women should recognize that Deborah, Esther, Rebecca, Miriam and Ruth will join women like Sarah (*I Peter 3:*) and Rahab in positions of leadership. The careful study of their lives is an interesting, truly fascinating, insight into the qualities of leadership that women can develop.

Matthew 22:3 shows that the resurrected immortals of God's kingdom are neither male nor female. Every leader, man or woman, which God uses in His kingdom will have been carefully schooled in the seven laws of success. These will be among the first things that all human beings are taught. Those who eventually grow into the low-level positions of human leadership will first learn to employ these laws. What politician of today has been taught the seven laws of success? How many have, from birth, been taught how to lead human beings toward good and right ends? What academy or institution has stood the test of time, having consistently trained people in matters of spiritual knowledge and understanding,

God's true character and principles, ethics and integrity? None!

The politicians and leaders of this world have practiced personal ambition, selfishness, greed, scheming, compromising, corruption, deception, and more, to get to the top. These qualities could not possibly qualify them for even greater leadership in the world tomorrow. In fact, these character deficiencies disqualify them in every regard. Yet such men will not readily admit or even see they are completely unfit to remain in office at the time of Christ's Return.

Not Given a Choice

The world's leaders and masses will not be *asked* if they *want* to obey God. They will *not* want to (*Romans 8:*). There will be no selling, cajoling, begging, beseeching, crying, pleading, whining or wheedling, to convince people that they need to be "saved". Christ will not *ask* world leaders if they will permit Him to replace them and their governments with His own. He will announce what is happening *to* them.

What world leader would *voluntarily* give up power? None! They will have to be *forcibly* removed. Leaders will be told that they are not, and have never been, properly qualified to lead. Nations will not voluntarily turn over the reins of power to a world government. This is part of the reason the nations will fight Christ at His Return. Consider: Would democratic governments, those ruling by the will of the people, readily accept or eagerly welcome government authority from the top down? Obviously not! Dictators might be happy with the *form* of hierarchical government from Jerusalem, but only if *they* were permitted to hold the power.

No, the world will not warmly receive Christ's rule and neither will Satan. The devil took mankind captive in the Garden of Eden. They have been his prisoners, his hostages, ever since. Christ will not come as some kind of top-flight "hostage negotiator," who will try to reason with the devil about why he should step down for the good of the world. He will forcibly remove him, and do so for the good of the world. For this same reason, the world's own good, Christ will literally seize all power and administer it in justice, equity and fairness for all.

What a glorious time that will be! What a magnificent, dazzling, shimmering jewel will be this marvelous new world. May we all pray *"Thy kingdom come,"* as we meditate on this coming, wonderful, utopian civilization!

Chapter V: Tomorrow's Wonderful World!

Before we can fully grasp what lies ahead in tomorrow's wonderful world, there is much more to consider. God has given us many additional details that offer direct insight into conditions during Christ's millennial rule. God has left nothing to chance. He prophesied thousands of years ago what the world to come will be like. Let's take some time to examine a few of the other details of what God's Word promises for this new, future world.

We have seen that, for now, crime and violence, pollution, poverty, illiteracy, war, famine, disease and ill health, and overpopulation stalk the earth as insoluble problems, growing ever worse. The greatest of these is overpopulation. Like smog over a great city, the world is choking under the growing weight of increasing numbers of human beings. While the population is growing, the planet is not. Neither is the amount of available food and water. At the same time that pollution is actually strangling and *reducing* their supply, demand for them *increases*.

God's Solution

It is beyond the scope of this book to address the last stages of God's Plan to save every human being that has *ever* lived from the time of Adam. Yet that is His purpose. At the end of Christ's 1,000-year rule, all these vast billions will be resurrected to physical life and given an opportunity to receive salvation. The earth must be ready to receive them.

God has a plan to prepare and reclaim potentially available land, in such vast expanses, that this problem will be solved for all time. Catastrophic prophesies, to be fulfilled just prior to Christ's Return, will bring unparalleled devastation and destruction to the earth's surface. God is most specific about what will happen. Weapons of mass destruction will be unleashed before, and possibly during, Christ's Coming. The "waste places" spoken of above may include nuclear "dead zones". Biological and nerve weapon releases may leave vast areas uninhabitable. God will have to literally *rehabilitate* the surface of the earth in order to make it fit, once again, for human habitation. Bear in mind that 77 percent of the earth's surface is already uninhabitable oceans and seas. Enormous deserts and great mountain ranges occupy a large percentage of earth's landmasses, including islands. Some regions of land (the two Poles) are too cold to inhabit. Only about 10 percent of the earth's surface is suitable for agriculture, with no more than 15 percent inhabitable.

God has a Master Plan. No man could ever think of it, or bring it to pass if he did. Yet it will solve *every* problem related to overpopulation, pollution, and production, procurement and distribution of food and water. It will involve a complete change in entire weather patterns around the earth, including ocean currents, jet streams and flow of arctic air. Beautiful, clear water will be available, in abundance, in all parts of the world. The nature of mountain ranges, islands and even the placement of continents will allow a repopulation of earth simply inconceivable to modern planners of cities and nations.

Deserts Disappear - Water Plentiful

The world is now running out of fresh drinking water, but that will soon change dramatically. Here is one of the most incredible prophecies in the entire Bible: *"Then shall the lame man leap...and the...dumb sing: for in the wilderness shall waters break out, and streams in the desert. And the parched ground shall become a pool, and the thirsty land springs of water: in the habitation of dragons, where each lay, shall be grass with reeds and rushes"* (*Isaiah 35:6-7*).

In tomorrow's world, the earth will be healed, resulting in beautiful landscapes, including deserts blossoming into verdant parks. Isaiah 35:1-2 add more to what this will mean for all the deserts of the world: *"The wilderness and the solitary place shall be glad for them; and the desert shall rejoice, and blossom as the rose. It shall blossom abundantly, and rejoice even with joy and singing: the glory of Lebanon shall be given unto it, the excellency of Carmel and Sharon, they shall see the glory of the Lord, and the excellency of our God."* Take time to read the entire 35th chapter of *Isaiah*.

The following is a phenomenal prophecy about a river that does not yet exist. It will flow from Jerusalem, in what will no doubt be the largest natural spring in the world, eventually reaching around the world: *"And it shall be in that day, that living waters shall go out from Jerusalem; half of them toward the former sea, and half of them toward the hinder sea: in summer and in winter shall it be"* (*Zechariah 14:8*). Wastelands of sand and cactus will break forth into a scenic beauty of lush greenery that is hard to imagine. Pasturelands, trees, shrubs, brooks, streams, rivers and gardens will replace all the deserts of the world.

But it is not just the deserts that will radically change in tomorrow's world.

Mountains Altered

Take a moment to savor the meaning pictured in this related prophecy, also in *Isaiah*. Notice what will happen to the mountains: *"Fear not, you worm Jacob, and you men of Israel; I will help you, says the Lord, and your Redeemer, the Holy One of Israel. Behold, I will make you a new sharp threshing instrument having teeth: you shall thresh the mountains, and beat them small, and shall make the hills as chaff. You shall fan them, and the wind shall carry them away, and the whirlwind shall scatter them: and you shall rejoice in the Lord, and shall glory in the Holy One of Israel. When the poor and needy seek water, and there is none, and their tongue fails for thirst, I the Lord will hear them, I the God of Israel will not forsake them. I will open rivers in high places, and fountains in the midst of the valleys: I will make the wilderness a pool of water, and the dry land springs of water. I will plant in the wilderness the cedar, the shittah tree, and the myrtle, and the oil tree; I will set in the desert the fir tree, and the pine, and the box tree together: That they may see, and know, and consider, and understand together, that the hand of the Lord has done this, and the Holy One of Israel has created it"* (*Isaiah 41:14-20*). Can you imagine this happening around the world? Mountains and hills will be shred like mulch, bubbling springs and new rivers will appear suddenly, and wilderness areas will disappear and be replaced by great forests of diverse trees. God says to "see," "know," "consider" and "understand" the scope of what He promises.

How awesome are the ways of God! This amazing prophecy depicts a world with plenty of room for people and their cities, parks, forests, recreation areas and crops as well as lakes and rivers. The biggest problem might be where to store the gargantuan food reserves that could soon appear. This would be a much better "problem" than the food wars that numerous experts predict will come, if something does not happen soon. Incidentally, do not forget that millions of pounds of beef on the hoof will be available in places like India, once superstition and ignorance is replaced by cooperation and *true* knowledge. So will the 50 percent of India's crops that are lost annually during the typhoon/monsoon season.

Why should Isaiah's prophecy seem strange? God's purpose has always been that people be happy and peaceful, contented and joyful. While this is strange and unusual in *this* world, it is neither strange nor unusual to

God. This is what He always intended for His creation. He wanted Adam and Eve to enjoy the garden that they eventually had to be expelled from. Since God formed the mountains (*Psalms 90:2; Amos 4:13*), He can also *re*-form them in any way that He wishes. He apparently will use great earthquakes to do much of the work (*Zechariah 14:4; Revelations 16:18*), because He states, *"The mountains quake at Him, and the hills melt"* (*Nahum 1:5*). *Isaiah 40:4* states, *"Every valley shall be exalted, and every mountain and hill shall be made low: and the crooked shall be made straight, and the rough places plain."* There are many great mountain ranges on earth. Imagine the desolate, snow-covered, windswept stretches of the Himalayas, Alps, Rockies, Andes, Hindu Cush, Sierras, Pyrenees and other great mountain ranges lowered or leveled and made fertile and inhabitable. Then picture the vast icepacks and mountain ranges of Antarctica, Greenland and Siberia, including immense areas of tundra and permafrost, becoming available. Countless millions of acres will be made available to a mankind, which could never do this for itself. Could all the nuclear weapons on earth blast away even a few of the world's great mountains? And what would remain if they could?

Now imagine how *many* great deserts would disappear. Start with much of the Middle East and almost all of Northern Africa. Picture the Sahara in Africa and nearly all of Saudi Arabia becoming lush and verdant. Then picture the Gobi desert in Asia and the Kalahari and Lake Chad basin, also of Africa, suddenly turning green, along with much of the American West and Southwest. More countless millions of acres of virtually useless land will become available for multiple purposes. Astonishing, but true; and in your lifetime!

Land and Wealth Beneath the Sea!

The oceans represent another growing threat to many of the coastal areas of the world. The relentless pounding of waves and tidal action, coupled with the rise of the oceans due to the now almost universally recognized onset of global warming, is creating a never-before-seen threat to the beaches and properties that they assault. But the oceans do not have to be destructive.

Vast untapped mineral wealth is available both in the ocean itself and beneath the ocean floor. However, it is now inaccessible to man. God promises that huge reserves of gold, silver, minerals and oil will soon be available. So will the water itself. Desalinization is now far too expensive, but only if man has to do it with no help. It would seem probable

that God's plan to increase the waters of earth, available for drinking, etc., will include some kind of plan for desalinization of part of the oceans. We know that God intends to shrink them in size. Notice: *"And the Lord shall utterly destroy the tongue of the Egyptian sea; and with His mighty wind shall He shake His hand over the river, and shall smite it in the seven streams, and make men go over dryshod"* (*Isa. 11:15*). Just as Holland ("hollow land"), through a vast network of dikes and canals, has reclaimed vast areas that were once under the sea, so will other nations do the same. Again, this will happen in your lifetime. Much fresh water will appear, along with gentle rains in due season. Too much water, in the form of devastating killer floods and the drowning of crops, will become a thing of the past. It has always been the case that while many areas do not have enough water, other areas have way too much. Man has never had a way of resolving this imbalance,
God does.

The Problem of Disease

As mentioned, every form of illness, sickness and pestilence stalks the earth. New diseases, and threats of epidemics, loom over large areas of the planet. Disease is as inseparable from mankind's history as is violence and war. But God never intended this (*III John 2*).

Recall that, after creating Adam and Eve, He said that all of His creation was *"very good"* (*Genesis 1:31*). This hardly leaves room for God having placed hidden, inactive viruses and bacteria within their bodies, waiting for the right moment to afflict them with horrible sickness and disease of every kind. Man is feverishly seeking to conquer disease. Yet he falls further and further behind. Just as we seem to control one disease, two more appear. This will all soon change. All man's efforts to cure diabetes, arthritis, cancer, heart disease, blindness, deafness, Alzheimer's, other diseases of the mind, strokes, AIDS, and a host of infant and childhood diseases will soon be unnecessary. All of the ongoing searches for new wonder drugs, treatments, specialized diagnoses, surgeries and procedures, advancements in technology, and every other kind of medical advancement, will soon be called off. God has always been the only One who can truly cure or heal all forms of sickness and disease (*Exodus 15:26; Psalms. 103:3*). This is because God alone has the ability to forgive sin, which is directly related to why people get sick (*Matthew 9:1-6; Psalms 41:3-4*). Mankind is now under the death penalty for sin (*Romans 6:23*). Often, death comes long before the end of a full lifetime, because men have not understood that God is Supreme Healer. They have not understood that *"by [Christ's] stripes you are healed"* (*I Peter 2:24*). This is because He *"took our infirmities, and bare our sicknesses"* (*Matthew 8:16-17*). When physical or spiritual laws have been broken, only God has the power to forgive.

Mass Global Healing

Earlier, we discussed the great law of *cause and effect*. Ignorance of this law has everything to do with why people get sick. Proper diet, sufficient water, sleep, fresh air, exercise, healthy thoughts and other important principles and laws form the basis of good health. People violate these in route to the bad effects, which we call disease. Modern medical schools acknowledge that they spend almost no time discussing the *prevention* of disease, but rather its *treatment* after it is present. Mankind will be taught that an ounce of prevention equals a pound of cure; individually and for all nations collectively. We previously discussed that right education would be incomplete without teaching humanity that good health is one of the laws to success.

In tomorrow's world people will be universally taught that *"sin is the transgression of the law"* (*I John 3:4*). We have discussed God's great spiritual laws, but He has numerous *physical* laws as well. Mankind has specialized in how to break them all. He is surrounded, therefore, by every kind of bad physical effect. Rampant disease and illness are among the greatest. Savor God's promise regarding the disappearance of disease and sickness in the world tomorrow and what makes this possible: *"But there the glorious Lord will be unto us a place of broad rivers and streams; wherein shall go no galley with oars, neither shall gallant ship pass thereby. For the Lord is our Judge, the Lord is our Lawgiver, the Lord is our King; He will save us...And the inhabitant shall not say, I am sick: the people that dwell therein shall be forgiven their iniquity"* (*Isaiah 33:21-22, 24*). This is just one passage proving that the removal of sickness requires the forgiveness of sin, "iniquity" or lawlessness. Here is an even more explicit promise from God, carrying additional details of the scope of mass healings to occur worldwide: *"Strengthen you the weak hands, and confirm the feeble knees. Say to them that are of a fearful heart, Be strong, fear not: behold, your God will come with vengeance, even God with a recompense; He will come and save you. Then the eyes of the blind shall be opened, and the ears of the deaf shall be unstopped. Then shall the lame man leap as an hart, and the tongue of the dumb sing..."* (*Isaiah 35:3-6*). There is coming a worldwide mass "healing revival." Only this one will be genuine, not one of fraud, mixed with pageantry and designed for television in order to "take in" many hopeful sufferers. Yes, mass healings would certainly be necessary, if God's planned utopian world were to produce the universal happiness, contentment and prosperity He has purposed.

No universal healing would be complete without God healing all of the diseased minds now clouded with every conceivable kind of mental illness and insanity. This scourge has plagued individuals, families and nations for millennia. Perfect mental health will be enjoyed by everyone; and all psychiatrists, psychologists, therapists, psychoanalysts and modern "shrinks" will be forced to find other work. How exciting to picture millions of blind people seeing sunsets that they had only heard described before and the deaf able to hear beautiful music, birds singing, and the sound of their children's voices. The joyful exuberance of some will be so great that the dumb will not just talk, they will *sing*! The lame will not just walk, they will *leap*!

Cities and Farmlands Also Healed

Why should it be that men do not understand that God wants to bless them? He is the Mastergiver of perfect gifts (*James 1:17*). God explained this to Israel and told them what obedience would bring them: *"And it shall come to pass, if you shall hearken diligently unto the voice of the Lord your God, to observe and to do all his commandments which I command you this day, that the Lord your God will set you on high above all nations of the earth: And all these blessings shall come on you, and overtake you, if you shall hearken unto the voice of the Lord your God. Blessed shall you be in the city, and blessed shall you be in the field. Blessed shall be the fruit of your body, and the fruit of your ground, and the fruit of your cattle, the increase of your kine, and the flocks of your sheep. Blessed shall be your basket and your store"* (*Deuteronomy 28:1-5*). This promise will soon apply to the whole world.

Again, without radiant health, who could be truly happy? This is what God wants: *"For I will restore health unto you, and I will heal you of your wounds"* (*Jeremiah 30:17*). And further, *"Therefore they shall come and sing in the height of Zion, and shall flow together to the goodness of the Lord, for wheat, and for wine, and for oil, and for the young of the flock and of the herd: and their soul shall be as a watered garden; and they shall not sorrow any more at all. Then shall the virgin rejoice in the dance, both young men and old together: for I will turn their mourning into joy, and will comfort them, and make them rejoice from their sorrow. And I will satiate the soul of the priests with fatness, and My people shall be satisfied with My goodness, says the Lord" (Jeremiah 31:12-14).* This picture is a far cry from what billions of people endure today, jammed together in cities full of pollution, pornography, crime, graffiti, litter, broken glass, excessive noise, blight, racial strife, exploding illegitimate births in one-parent homes, misery and poverty.

Cities are not now blessed, they are *cursed* with every conceivable ill and evil!

Universal Safety and Security

The streets of cities around the world will soon be safe for all. Look at this description of how Jerusalem, certainly one of the most violent, unsafe cities on earth today, will change: *"There shall yet old men and old women dwell in the streets of Jerusalem, and every man with his staff in his hand for very age. And the streets of the city shall be full of boys and girls playing in the streets thereof" (Zechariah 8:4-5).* Abandoned buildings, choking traffic, drug dealers, the homeless, street gangs, criminals, and all fear will soon only be memories. How ironic that God will have to force a rebellious mankind to receive His blessings and enjoy health, well-being, joy, and compulsory happiness

Even animals will no longer be a threat. Their nature will be completely changed in a stunning way. Picture this: *"The wolf also shall dwell with the lamb, and the leopard shall lie down with the kid; and the calf and the young lion and the fatling together; and a little child shall lead them. And the cow and the bear shall feed; their young ones shall lie down together: and the lion shall eat straw like the ox. And the sucking child shall play on the hole of the asp, and the weaned child shall put his hand on the cockatrice' den (Isaiah 11:6-8).* Lions as pets? Wolves jumping through hoops on the front lawn? Tiny children "walking the leopard"? Babies playing with once-deadly snakes? It is all prophesied to happen. You could live to see it—and be part of teaching it to others if you believe and act on God's Word.

Here is a summary of God's overall promise to the inhabitants of earth: *"Then shall your light break forth as the morning, and your health shall spring forth speedily: and your righteousness shall go before you; the glory of the Lord shall be your rearward" (Isaiah 58:8).*

Nations Return to Homelands

Individual ethnic and racial groups will eventually be returned to their native lands.

First notice how God plans to repatriate the original Promised Land, once occupied by ancient Israel, with modern Israel. Then blessing them greatly after they arrive: *"For, behold, I am for you, and I will turn unto you, and you shall be tilled and sown: And I will multiply men upon you, all the house of Israel, even all of it: and the cities shall be inhabited, and the wastes shall be built: And I will multiply upon you man and beast; and they shall increase and bring fruit: and I will settle you after your old estates, and will do better unto you than at your beginnings: and you shall know that I am the Lord"* (*Ezekiel 36:9-11*). This is a wonderful picture of a complete renovation of the war-torn lands of the Middle East. Here is more: *"Thus says the Lord God; In the day that I shall have cleansed you from all your iniquities I will also cause you to dwell in the cities, and the wastes shall be built...And they shall say, This land that was desolate is become like the garden of Eden; and the waste and desolate and ruined cities are become fenced, and are inhabited"* (*Ezekiel 36:33, 35*). Finally, Isaiah states this: *"He shall cause them that come of Jacob to take root: Israel shall blossom and bud, and fill the face of the world with fruit"* (*Isaiah 27:6*).

But Israel will not be alone in this process. Her worst enemies, Germany and Egypt, are prophesied to dwell together with her in peace and cooperation. Notice: *"In that day shall there be a highway out of Egypt to Assyria [Germany], and the Assyrian shall come into Egypt, and the Egyptian into Assyria, and the Egyptians shall serve with the Assyrians. In that day shall Israel be the third with Egypt and with Assyria, even a blessing in the midst of the land: Whom the Lord of hosts shall bless, saying, Blessed be Egypt My people, and Assyria the work of My hands, and Israel Mine inheritance"* (*Isaiah 19:23-25*). What an incredible, staggering, prophecy this is!

Those who are now mortal enemies will enjoy complete peace, with commerce and travel occurring freely between these then cooperating nations. Business dealings in the world tomorrow will be based on honesty, trust, proper ethics, and outgoing concern for others.

The New World Economy

I have never met a single person who actually wished to be unhappy. All want to live life to the fullest, and feel happiness and joy. But most have simply not known how to do this. Almost no one understands that it is God's will that we *"prosper and be in health."* Notice what Christ told His disciples, and what He will one day tell the whole world: *"I am come that they might have life, and that they might have it more abundantly"* (*John 10:10*). Yes, God wants everyone to live rich, full, abundant lives.

He wants all peoples to enjoy His blessings. Savor this next wonderful verse: *"And in this mountain [God's government] shall the Lord of hosts make unto all people a feast of fat things, a feast of wines on the lees, of fat things full of marrow, of wines on the lees well refined. And He will destroy in this mountain the face of the covering cast over all people, and the veil that is spread over all nations"* (*Isaiah 25:6-7*). This passage reveals God's truly awesome Plan to bless all nations and remove the veil of blindness now covering them.

For 6,000 years, this veil has brought complete darkness to men's understanding. It has blinded his religions, governments, armies, cultures, educational systems, morality and values, family structures, methods of commerce, approach to disease and ill heath, management of the planet's resources, approach to problem-solving, how he resolves conflicts, his international relations and more.

Abundant Blessings

We saw that the survivors of Israel will be returned to their homeland. Once there, they will be blessed with abundance. God will cause the other nations to support Israel, to lavish wealth and gifts upon them and to serve their needs.

God tells them at this time: *"Lift up your eyes round about, and see: all they gather themselves together, they come to you: your sons shall come from far, and your daughters shall be nursed [carried or supported] at your side. Then you shall see, and flow together, and your heart shall fear, and be enlarged; because the abundance of the sea shall be converted unto you, the forces [wealth] of the Gentiles shall come unto you. The multitude of camels shall cover you, the dromedaries of Midian and Ephah; all they from Sheba shall come: they shall bring gold and in-*

cense; and they shall show forth the praises of the Lord" (*Isaiah 60:4-6*). This shows that these physical Israelites will be overwhelmed with all the abundance with which God blesses them. Not only will Jerusalem become the headquarters of the government of God, it will become the financial headquarters of the world.

As the topography of the earth is changed through the series of earthquakes that occur in the traumatic times surrounding the Return of Christ, vast reserves of valuable minerals hidden in the earth will be made accessible for the first time. This would include precious metals, raw materials and petroleum reserves needed for certain industries that will exist in tomorrow's civilization. The scripture cited above also indicated that *"the abundance of the sea shall be converted unto you [Israel]."* Man's technology in the past few decades has given him the capability of positively identifying many specific minerals and elements in the seas by using modern technology called chemical spectroscopy. Many of these minerals are already being extracted from seawater by advanced chemical techniques. Yet the technology to filter cubic miles of ocean water in order to extract significant amounts of the precious metals has not been developed. But all estimates are that the wealth of even a single cubic mile of seawater is simply enormous, measuring in the billions of dollars.

Although man can identify the oceans' precious elements, only God can extract great quantities from them. Truly, as the Psalm proclaims, *"The Lord is a great God, and a great King above all gods. In His hand are the deep places of the earth: the strength of the hills is His also. The sea is His, and He made it: and His hands formed the dry land"* (*Psalms 95:3-5*). As Creator of the entire universe, God can readily assemble the wealth of the earth to adorn Jerusalem and Israel as the physical and spiritual capital of the new world. Notice: *"For thus says the Lord of hosts; Yet once, it is a little while, and I will shake the heavens, and the earth, and the sea, and the dry land; And I will shake all nations, and the desire [Christ] of all nations shall come: and I will fill this house with glory, says the Lord of hosts. The silver is Mine, and the gold is Mine, says the Lord of hosts"* (*Haggai 2:6-8*). The breathtaking glittering beauty of the new world capital will far surpass even the glory of the temple and buildings of King Solomon's time.

Certainly the temple complex atop Mount Zion will be the most spectacular of all, with the three tower structures at each gate to the outer court matched by three more identical towers at each gate proceeding to the inner court. The greatest tower of the entire complex will extend above the porch at the temple entrance. The height of this structure will exceed a 25-story building, a majestic sight already atop Mount Zion, which will be elevated by that time. Of course, the two pillars of fine brass, on either side of the entrance and rising more than 50 feet into the air, will be truly awesome to see.

Sound Financial Policies

The new world economic system will be established upon sound fiscal policies. There will be no more profiteering from risky investments in the performance of other people or business concerns. There will be no more financial institutions, insurance companies and loan agencies, as we now know them. Banks will probably exist in some form, but with an interest in more than the profit motive.

Individuals will learn not to overspend. People will be encouraged to follow sound financial practices and to buy no more than they can realistically afford. There will be no flashy advertisements intended to induce lust to "buy now" in order to satisfy the instant gratification encouraged by all of today's advertising media. Rather, the established way will emphasize the work ethic, obedience to God's laws, and the way of give and outgoing concern toward others.

Also, by removing the commercial frenzy that accompanies the pagan holidays of this world, the worst inducement for overspending, often far beyond one's means, will be eliminated. Of course, the knowledge of the true Holy Days will be taught and practiced throughout the world. Some will resist the observance of these Holy Days at first: *"And it shall be, that whoso will not come up of all the families of the earth unto Jerusalem to worship the King, the Lord of hosts, even upon them shall be no rain. And if the family of Egypt go not up, and come not, that have no rain; there shall be the plague, wherewith the Lord will smite the heathen that come not up to keep the feast of tabernacles"* (*Zechariah 14:17-18*). In short order, the whole world will be keeping God's Holy Days in place of the world's pagan holidays.

To survive in today's hostile world, governments must collect exorbitant rates of taxation to finance military forces and expanded law enforcement personnel. Of course, greed on the part of many government leaders accounts for much of the excess taxation that is now so burdensome to so many. As governments expand, they tend to extract more in taxes as a means to redistribute wealth, pursuing the socialistic philosophies that predominate in this world. Outrageous tax rates will be eliminated.

The administration of God's government has costs. However, instead of tax rates ranging from 30 to 90 percent God's government requires a tithe of just 10 percent! That 10 percent belongs to God (*Leviticus 27:30*). God views this command most seriously: *"Will a man rob God? Yet you have robbed Me. But you say, Wherein have we robbed You? In tithes and offerings. You are cursed with a curse: for you have robbed Me, even this whole nation. Bring you all the tithes into the storehouse, that there may be meat in Mine house, and prove Me now herewith, says the Lord of hosts, if I will not open you the windows of heaven, and pour you out a blessing, that there shall not be room enough to receive it"* (*Malachi 3:8-10*). Most nations have a variety of heavy, burdensome, hidden taxes, and national health and social security services. Ever-mounting taxes become overwhelming to many now struggling to survive. These burdens will be lifted in tomorrow's world.

Through proper re-education of the world, God's laws of health will become known, and compliance with them will become practical and affordable. Transportation and other logistical issues will be solved so that people will generally live in small enclaves and villages in agrarian settings. Living near one's work will become desirable, and possible.

Careful forethought and planning will insure that congestion and overcrowding do not threaten the peace and security of each family's living place: *"But they shall sit every man under his vine and under his fig tree; and none shall make them afraid: for the mouth of the Lord of hosts has spoken it"* (*Micah 4:4*).

A World in Harmony with God's Laws

Once people are living in obedience to God's laws and human nature has disappeared, the world will be vastly different.

With good weather everywhere, year-round, the devastating setbacks of this age will no longer occur. No more droughts, floods, tornadoes, hurricanes, earthquakes or other catastrophic forms of weather will be reported. There will be no more human tragedies involving alcohol, drugs, gambling or other devastating addictions. How will this change be brought to pass? Those who are immortal spirit beings in the God Family will always be present to insure that everyone understands when, where

94

and how to obey God.

Safety, peace, cooperation and strong family ties will define the world tomorrow. Notice: *"And though the Lord give you the bread of adversity, and the water of affliction, yet shall not your teachers be removed into a corner any more, but your eyes shall see your teachers: And your ears shall hear a word behind you, saying, This is the way, walk you in it, when you turn to the right hand, and when you turn to the left"* (*Isaiah 30:20-21*). Imagine what the world will be like when everyone listens to their teachers and keeps *all* of the Ten Commandments. Here is a brief description of how obeying each of the commandments will bring great blessings:

- As the world begins to keep the first commandment (*no other gods* before the true God) there will not be anymore false religions. When the world comes to know and to fear *this* God, it will learn that His system of government and education yields the way to *true* peace, joy and *real* fulfillment. The world will come to appreciate and obey the other nine commandments. Upon seeing the majesty of the glorified Jesus Christ, the masses will recognize that their religions deceived them and proclaim, *"O Lord, my strength, and my fortress, and my refuge in the day of affliction, the Gentiles shall come unto You from the ends of the earth, and shall say, Surely our fathers have inherited lies, vanity, and things wherein there is no profit"* (*Jeremiah 16:19*).
- As the world comes to keep the second commandment (turning from the worship of graven images, pictures, and *idolatry*) the terrible curses brought on the world because of this superstitious ignorance will cease.
- Then as the world practices the third commandment (*not taking God's name in vain*) profanity, euphemisms, and vain phrases will vanish. This also includes such practices as vain repetition in prayer (*Matthew 6:7*).
- Obedience to the fourth commandment (keeping *the Sabbath* holy) will greatly benefit all mankind. By observing God's weekly Sabbath and annual Holy Days, they stand or fall together .Everyone will learn of the true God and His Master Plan, depicted by these days. The Sabbath is the identifying sign between God and His people. It is the great *test commandment*. Those who delight in God's Sabbath will be blessed. God promises that they will *"ride upon the high places of the earth"* and *"be fed with the heritage of Jacob [promised birthright*

blessings] your father" (*Isaiah 58:14*).

- As all children of the world learn to obey the fifth commandment (*honoring parents*) they also learn to more easily honor God. Reform schools and youth detention centers will disappear, as will all juvenile courts. Respect for the elderly, as well as for all authority and teachers, will replace them. As a direct result of honoring their parents, young people are promised long lives. Since they will also be taught to be useful and productive, this will be a great blessing.

- By obeying the sixth commandment (*not killing*) threats of nuclear, chemical, or biological attacks cease to exist. Imagine no fear of nuclear warfare or terrorist attacks by mad fanatics. The defense budgets of many nations, which usually comprise the largest portion of their gross national product, will be diverted to more productive uses. It can be spent helping people learn how to truly better their lives. Obedience to this commandment will also bring an end to homicides, suicides, abortions, hate, malice, bitterness, all forms of slander, character assassination, and other sorts of malicious will.

- As the world begins to keep the seventh commandment (*not committing adultery*) people will consider the long-term consequences of their actions. Without the influence of Satan, who motivates the sex-driven media, the obsession with sex will yield to God's wholesome way of living, without the curses and setbacks of adultery. Pornography, pedophilia, illegitimate births, perversity and sexually transmitted diseases will be cursed by-products of a past degenerate age.

- When the world keeps the eighth commandment (*not stealing*) locks will no longer be necessary. Armored cars and armed guards will no longer be seen. Without theft, robbery, and shoplifting, prices at shops and stores will not have to reflect what retailers call "shrinkage." Honesty by employers and employees will be a welcome relief, and strangers will no longer be suspected of intent to rob or harm.

- Obedience to the ninth commandment (*not lying or bearing false witness*) will allow people to begin to trust what others say. No longer will politicians and world leaders promote false distortions and propaganda to advance their own agenda. All slander and character assassination of opponents will cease, partly because there will be no such thing as political opponents. People will be known for what they are, rather than the false perceptions from malicious slander and gossip. There will be no false fronts to deceive others.

- Finally, as the world keeps the tenth commandment (*not coveting*) there will be no more lust and covetousness to allure people to commit idolatry, fornication and adultery. People will also learn that the goal of being rich is destructive (*I Timothy 6:9-10*). They will learn that giving to others always returns even greater blessings to the giver (*Luke 6:38*). They will learn that putting their treasure in heaven is their greatest investment (*Matthew 6:19-20*). Lust-driven consumerism will also disappear, along with overwhelming consumer debt and resulting bankruptcy. Without lust, materialism and impulse buying will vanish.

Now notice this promise of another change to come: *"The vile person shall be no more called liberal [generous], nor the churl [modern athletes, rock stars, entertainers and others] said to be bountiful. For the vile person will speak villany, and his heart will work iniquity, to practice hypocrisy, and to utter error against the Lord, to make empty the soul of the hungry, and He will cause the drink of the thirsty to fail"* (*Isaiah 32:5-6*). What will tomorrow be like? With God's government ruling mankind and right education the result will be peace, safety, prosperity and abundance for all.

A Truly Wonderful World

Tomorrow's wonderful world will *be* wonderful because of the presence of the King, Jesus Christ, and the resurrected members of the God Family who assist Him. It will be wonderful because the whole world will keep and uphold the laws of God. All peoples will learn to put God first in their lives in *everything*; including learning to always seek the kingdom of God above every other goal (*Matthew 6:31-33*).

There will be absolutely no exceptions for those who may wish to rebel and serve other gods. Notice this: *"For it is written, As I live, says the Lord, every knee shall bow to Me, and every tongue shall confess to God"* (*Romans 14:11*). Mankind will live in complete harmony with his Creator and with all peoples in tomorrow's wonderful world. All will learn to say, *"We give You thanks, O Lord God Almighty, which are, and was, and are to come; because You have taken to You Your great power, and have reigned"* (*Revelations 11:17*). God speed this day!

The Big Picture

At the conclusion of his book *"The WONDERFUL WORLD TOMOR-ROW; What It Will Be Like"*, Herbert W. Armstrong wrote this dazzling, marvelous description of Tomorrow's World under the subhead "The Final Summation":

"Statesmen, scientists, educators know the only hope for survival and for peace is one world government. We could quote many scores of world leaders affirming this.

We could quote other scores of world leaders saying it is impossible.

So it's 'world government—or annihilation' on the one hand, and it's 'world government is impossible' on the other hand.

"That is the stark paradox of terror facing all mankind today. No wonder God Almighty says *'the way of peace have they not known'* (*Romans 3:1*).

But what man cannot do for himself, the Great Living God will do for him. World government—perfect government—is coming in our time, in the hands of the Great Ruling Christ, and unnumbered thousands of Co-Rulers given immortality with and under Him.

And that good news is the true Gospel of Jesus Christ. Christ is to inherit the world throne (*Luke 1:32-3*), which God had promised to David would never cease on this earth (*II Samuel 7:1*). Jesus said, before Pilate, it was for this express purpose that He was born (*John 18:36-3*).

Jesus constantly preached the good news about the coming Kingdom of God (*Matthew 4:2; 6:1; 7:2; Mark 1:1; 4:1; 14:2; Luke 4:4; 8:1; 9:, 1, 6, etc.*). He pictured Himself as the young nobleman going away (to heaven) to be coronated, and to return to earth (*Luke 19:12-2*).

Repeatedly Jesus said He would return to earth (*Matthew 24:2, 30-3, 4; 25:1; Mark 13:2; Luke 12:42-4; 17:2; 18:; 19:1; 21:2; John 14:, etc.*). *'If I go and prepare a place [position, office, habitation] for you, I will come again, and receive you unto myself, that where I am, there ye may be also'* (*John 14:*). He will then be on the earth—compare *Zechariah 14:3-* with *I Thessalonians 4:1*.

The living Christ is coming in all the power and glory of Almighty God, as *'King of kings and Lord of lords'* (*Revelation 19:11-2*), to put down the rebellion of warring nations (*Revelation 17:1*), and establish God's world-ruling Government over all nations (*Daniel 2:4; 7:, 13-1, 1, 2, 2; Isaiah 9:*).

No wonder the whole hope of a true Christian is the resurrection (*Acts 23:; 24:1*) to immortality—eternal life—as a co-ruler, under Christ. Jesus said: *'And he that overcometh, and keepeth my works unto the end, to him will I give power over the nations: and he shall rule them with a rod of iron...'* (*Revelation 2:26-2*). And again, *'to him that overcometh will I grant to sit with me in my throne [on this earth]...'* (*Revelation 3:2; Luke 1:32-3*). And *'...we shall reign on the earth'* (*Revelation 5:1*).

The Apostle John, in vision, saw a preview of the beginning of that rule and world government: *'And I saw thrones, and they sat upon them, and judgment was given unto them...and they lived and reigned with Christ a thousand years'* (*Revelation 20:*).

Jesus said no one could see or enter into the Kingdom of God until he is born of God (*John 3:3-*). He made plain when one is born of God, he, just as God is, will be Spirit. We have now, as humans, been born of flesh—and therefore we are flesh. But God is Spirit (*John 4:2, Revised Standard Version*), and when we are born of God—of the Spirit—we shall be Spirit (*John 3:6-*). Now, we are earthy—of the earth (*I Corinthians 15:4*). We are 'flesh and blood' from the earth—from matter (*verse 5*)—yet flesh and blood humans cannot inherit the Kingdom of God (*same verse*). But, as we have borne the image of the earthy—mortal—human—we shall, when born of God, bear the image of the heavenly that is, spirit (*verse 4*).

Christ, the King of kings. Perfect in character, absolute in honesty, integrity, faithfulness, loyalty and trust; filled with outgoing concern for the governed—their welfare and salvation; total knowledge, understanding, wisdom. Complete love, mercy, patience, kindness, compassion, forgiveness. Yet, possessing total power, and never compromising one millionth of an inch with His perfect law—which is the way of love. He will enforce God's Law—God's Government on earth. He will compel haughty, carnal, rebellious humans to yield in complete submission to God's Government.

No one will be deceived—as the vast majority of mankind is today. All will know the truth. No more religious confusion. Eyes will be opened to the truth. Humans will become teachable. People will start living God's Way— the way of outgoing concern for others—the way of the true values—the way of peace, of happiness, of well-being, of joy.

Crime, sickness, disease, pain and suffering, gone. Poverty, ignorance banished. Smiles on people's faces—faces that radiate. Wild animals tame. Air pollution, water pollution, soil pollution, gone. Crystal pure water to drink; clean, crisp, pure air to breathe; rich black soil where deserts, mountains and seas formerly were, producing full-flavored foods, and fantastic beauty in flowers, shrubs, trees. A world filled with happy radiating humans, guided, helped, protected, and ruled by former mortals made immortal—and all the humans realizing that they, too, may inherit everlasting life in supreme happiness and thrilling joy.

What a fabulous picture!"

Epilogue: You Can Live the Abundant Life!

Never has the world had so much, yet been so miserable. Depression, unhappiness, confusion, frustration, unfulfilled hopes and dreams, dissatisfaction, emptiness, and hopeless misery describe humanity the world over.

The United States Constitution guarantees people the right to "life, liberty, and the pursuit of happiness." While the framers of the Constitution understood they could guarantee the American citizenry certain civil liberties and freedom from oppression, they understood they could not guarantee happiness. They could only seek to guarantee one's right to "pursue" it. Many are pursuing happiness, but in all the wrong places!

Vast new frontiers of expanding scientific knowledge have not brought the satisfaction and happiness that leaders prophesied would accompany this advancement. Neither have laborsaving devices, which were supposed to bring people more leisure time to "enjoy themselves." Instead, mental illness, drug addiction, despair, suicide, alcoholism, self-pity, other forms of escapism, and general discontent with life abound everywhere. Educators have failed to lead people to the abundant life. Like science and education, religion has also failed terribly in teaching people what God intends them to know about real abundant living. Many religions have taught people to feel guilty if they enjoy themselves. Most believe that God wants them to suppress joy and happiness, and that Christ expects this from His followers. Millions view Christianity as little more than a series of "Thou shalt nots," rather than as the path to enjoying a wonderful, abundant life. These same millions often think of sin as the fun that will end if they obey God. They think that "accepting Jesus" also means accepting a life of almost morbid gloom and doom.

Be honest with yourself. Haven't you seen Christianity primarily in this light? Haven't you thought that Christianity primarily means an end to fun, pleasure, excitement, thrills, and leading an interesting life? Haven't you also thought of most church services as solemn, sober, unemotional and devoid of real meaning and happiness? Because of this, many attend certain more emotional churches, seeking an emotional feeling (always temporary) that they equate with happiness, so that they can fill their terrible emptiness inside. All of this wrong understanding exists because almost no one equates Christianity with enjoying a true zest for life.

What Christ Said

On the last night before His crucifixion, Christ taught His disciples many vital principles. At one point, He said, *"These things have I spoken unto you, that My joy might remain in you, and that your joy might be full"* (*John 15:11*). On the same occasion, Christ, knowing the disciples would sorrow at His death, added, *"But your sorrow shall be turned into joy.... and your joy no man takes from you"* (*John 16:20, 22*). This is a powerful promise. Christians are to experience real joy and happiness in this life. If they are truly pleasing and obeying God, there is nothing that anyone can do to take this joy away.

This is an extraordinary statement. But most know nothing of it, or of other verses about this subject. Yet it has been God's purpose from the beginning that His servants enjoy life to the full. And God has also intended that His people enjoy life with His joy. Christ said *"My [His] joy"* was to remain with His disciples. Consider. The true God of the Bible is the happiest Being in the universe. David understood this: *"In Your [God's] presence is fullness of joy"* (*Psalms 16:11*). Do you see what David is saying? God intends that you live a life of full joy and happiness, His happiness. The very same kind of happiness that God Himself experiences. God lives life with "fullness of joy." All those in His presence experience it as well. The apostle Jude added that God wants *"to present you faultless before the presence of His glory with exceeding joy"* (*Jude 24*). This is your ultimate destiny!

Why then would God expect His people to merely endure this life? Yes, this life is a time of lesson-learning, including trials and suffering. But it is also a forerunner, in a very small way, of what eternal life is intended to be. It would make no sense for God to expect life to consist of only suffering and pain now as a preparation for perfect joy and happiness later.

What Christ Brought

Many years ago, I learned of one of the most incredible verses in the entire Bible. No one in the large, respected denomination of my youth ever spoke of it. Apparently, none ever thought about it either, because their lives did not reflect radiant happiness. Notice: *"I am come that they might have life, and that they might have it more abundantly"* (*John 10:10*). Have you ever seen, or even heard of, this passage before? Probably not! Christ came bringing the abundant life, and He said so plainly

101

Why then do so many believe that Christianity is supposed to be endured instead of enjoyed. Why do they not understand that the radiant, abundant life can be theirs—if they will follow God's formula to achieve it? This book merely explains how all nations will one day experience what individual true Christians now enjoy. God never instructs or commands His people to avoid anything unless it is for their own good. Many things seem like fun, but carry a delayed penalty, and terrible price, for having done them. God instructs us on what to avoid so that we will not get hit later by an unexpected "boomerang".

I have never met a single person who actually wanted to be unhappy. All want to live life to the fullest, and feel happiness and joy. But most have simply not known how to do this, or whether God even expected it. He does expect it, and even tells you how!

Introducing the Bible Formula

For every person, there is a different definition for what a Christian is. Do you know the definition? Are you sure? Can you turn to a single verse that explains this, removing all doubt?

There is such a verse, and it is the only place to begin to fully understand how to live the happy, joyful, abundant life. The apostle Paul probably said more about the subject of happiness than any other Bible writer. We will see some of these verses in a moment. But the verse that speaks most about this subject appears not to mention it. Notice: *"But you are not in the flesh, but in the Spirit, if so be that the Spirit of God dwell in you. Now if any man have not the Spirit of Christ, he is none of His"* (Romans 8:9). This basic scripture leaves no room for misunderstanding. A Christian is one who has the Spirit of God. If not, *"he is none of His."* This includes you. Countless millions of professing Christians sincerely believe that they are "Christ's." Yet they do not have God's Spirit and are, therefore, not Christians at all.

Let's keep this simple, and move step-by-step. The beginning point of Christianity is that one must receive the Holy Spirit. But what does this mean? What does having the Spirit of God have to do with happiness, joy, and the abundant life? Let's see more of why *Romans 8:9* has much to do with this subject. Paul wrote the Galatians, *"But the fruit of the Spirit is love, joy, peace, longsuffering, gentleness, goodness, faith, meekness, temperance ..."* (*Galatians 5:22-23*). This verse is all-important. When a newly converted Christian receives the Spirit of God, he receives a little of each of these qualities of God's character. We have already seen that God experiences fullness of joy, so it is not strange then that His Holy Spirit, which is His *"divine nature"* (*2 Peter 1:4*), includes joy.

- The Christian starts out by practicing love, which is the only fruit listed before joy. Love is the fulfilling of the Law of God (*Romans 13:10; 1 John 5:3*).
- "Joy" is listed second because it is the first and most immediate by-product of practicing obedience to God's Law.
- Next comes "peace," which flows from being genuinely happy in life, and happy toward those around you.

It is not hard to see how this will yield real peace in your relationships with others. Without the presence of God's Spirit within one's mind, which produces the deep, inner peace that Paul wrote must *"rule in your hearts"* (*Colossians. 3:15*), it is impossible to be happy. Each of the fruits of the Spirit following peace will flow as a direct result of having the Spirit of God, and being a real Christian. While millions may think that they are Christians, and may think that they have the Spirit of God, they have not followed the biblical formula (*Acts 2:38*).

This means you. If you have God's Spirit present within you, you can experience both a joy and peace that no one can take from you, even when you are persecuted. Paul wrote, *"... all that will live godly in Christ Jesus shall suffer persecution"* (*2 Timothy 3:12*). So you will be perse-cuted for your beliefs, but this need not upset you and cause unhappiness. God actually tells us to *"rejoice, and be exceeding glad"* (*Matthew 5:11-12*) when the very worst and most intense kinds of persecution and false accusation are thrown against us. This is because we will receive a *"great[er] reward"* at Christ's Return, as a result.

A Man of Sorrows, But Happy

The same is true of enduring trials, which are a part of every Christian's life. Christ was not an exception when it came to trials and suffering. We have seen that He experienced joy and left it with His disciples and with His Church, through His Spirit given on Pentecost (*Acts 2*). Yet Christ was also *"a man of sorrows [pain], and acquainted with grief"* (*Isaiah 53:3*).

How could it be both? How could Christ be full of joy and experience a life of sorrows and grief? Overcoming and conquering sin is not easy. Christ conquered sin, so He understood this. He knew that the whole world lives in sin and suffers terribly as a result. This brought Him great sorrow because it was never what He intended for mankind. Christ also understood that the Christian way involves trials and difficulties throughout life. This is an inescapable fact for those in whom God is working. These are essential to the character-building process, and are good for us. Trials and tests can make us temporarily sorrowful, but bring great joy when we understand their purpose. Here is how the apostle Peter told us to view trials: *"Beloved, think it not strange concerning the fiery trial which is to try you, as though some strange thing happened unto you: but rejoice, inasmuch as you are partakers of Christ's sufferings; that, when His glory shall be revealed, you may be glad also with exceeding joy"* (*1 Peter 4:12-13*). No one likes to suffer. Certainly Christ did not look forward to pain and suffering. But He knew, as He endured these things, that He would soon be sitting at God's right hand, restored to full glory.

During trials we are to focus on the glorious reward, ruling with Christ in tomorrow's wonderful world, that awaits us, if we *"endure unto the end"* (*Matthew 24:13)* throughout this life. Of course, most people do think that trials are "strange"; that they are bad, painful, and undesirable. They certainly are inconvenient. Most convince themselves that their trials are worse than everyone else's, but this is not true. Christians have to train themselves to recognize that trials bring lessons, and lessons learned forge, temper, and strengthen one's character. This is why the apostle James instructed, *"Count it all joy when you fall into various temptations [trials]; knowing this, that the trying of your faith works patience"* (*James 1:2-3)*. Temptations are tests. And so are trials. God says to count these opportunities for building character as a time for *"joy"*. Again, why? Because of the "exceeding joy" that we shall have when Christ returns. And we will receive a greater reward because of more character that has been built.

Peter also wrote, *"Wherein you greatly rejoice, though now for a season, if need be, you are in heaviness through manifold temptations: that the trial of your faith, being much more precious than of gold that perishes, though it [our character] be tried with fire, might be found unto praise and honor and glory at the appearing of Jesus Christ"* (*1 Peter 1:6-7)*. Peter added, *"Blessed be the God and Father of our Lord Jesus Christ, which according to His abundant mercy has begotten us again unto a lively hope by the resurrection of Jesus Christ from the dead, to an in-heritance incorruptible, and undefiled.... unto salvation ready to be re-vealed in the last time"* (*1 Peter 1:3-5*). Is this now clear? Do you see the direct connection to trials now and greater reward later, leading in tomor-row's world? No wonder God says we should be joyful during trials, temptations, and persecutions.

Now you know what to do the next time you experience trials and diffi-culties. Do not become unhappy, wondering what is wrong, and moan, groan, and complain as though something bad has happened. Instead, re-alize it is something that is very good, IF received and used properly. Why, if you are building something "more precious than gold," would you complain or feel unhappy about it?

Christianity Means Change

Becoming a Christian means a total change to a completely different way of life. It means a whole different way of thinking and believing. You must recognize that people do not automatically understand all God's ways at the outset of conversion. All wrong ways, values, and beliefs must be unlearned, and everything that is good, pure, and right, all things of God, must be learned!

God says, *"For my thoughts are not your thoughts, neither are your ways my ways, says the Lord. For as the heavens are higher than the earth, so are My ways higher than your ways, and My thoughts than your thoughts"* (*Isaiah 55:8-9*). This scripture is profound and far-reaching in meaning. It involves everything we think, say, and do, including how we view the subject of joy, happiness, and living the abundant life. It means recognizing that this is what God wants. This may mean sweeping from your mind all previous false concepts of what you thought Christianity was supposed to be like. If you are Christ's, then your eyes are fixed on the kingdom of God (*Matthew 6:33*). You understand that this is the big-gest objective, the greatest goal, in your life. Never forget that everything in your life is subordinate to achieving salvation, and building character along the path to that end.

Pause and think for a moment. How many things could bring more peace and satisfaction than understanding why you were born and where your life is going? The excitement, joy, thrill, and enormous contentment that flow from this confident assurance will dwarf every trial, difficulty, hur-dle, obstacle, and problem you will ever face in your life. If you truly grasp this statement, you have gone a long way toward comprehending why Christ said that His way represents a life more wonderful, more abundant, than most could ever imagine.

Serving God does not mean a loss of fun and giving up pleasures but rather understanding what real fun and real pleasures are, and enjoying them.

Putting God First

Let's take a moment to read *Matthew 6:33: "But seek you first the kingdom of God, and His righteousness; and all these things [material blessings] shall be added unto you."* John also wrote, *"Beloved, I wish above all things that you may prosper and be in health, even as your soul [life] prospers"* (3 John 2). These verses express God's will regarding receiving physical things, enjoying prosperity, in your life. In time, if you truly put God and His kingdom first, you have His sure promise that He will add physical, material, blessings to your life. It is impossible for God to lie (*Hebrews 6:18*). When He makes a promise, He keeps it, and He has promised you that *"these things"* will flow into your life, if you put Him first. You can count on this!

Malachi 3:8-10 is an example of how this principle works in the mind of God, how He views faithful obedience. When we obey Him, good things happen, and sometimes lots of good things. But be careful that you do not expect them right away. Also be careful that you do not obey God simply because "there is something (material) in it for you." Many Bible verses speak of the importance of being patient and waiting for answered prayers and blessings to come according to God's timetable.

Also, we must be sure that we are pleasing God as a regular practice in our lives. Let's read an important verse that ties obedience to confidence and answered prayer. John wrote, *"Beloved, if our heart [mind and conscience] condemn us not, then have we confidence toward God. And whatsoever we ask, we receive of Him, because we keep His commandments, and do those things that are pleasing in His sight"* (1 John 3:21-22). Take time to savor this verse. Internalize it, practice it, and then expect that God will give you all the physical things that you need.

Source of Enormous Power

Almost no one understands what Christianity really is. They have no idea that it can bring them supreme happiness, beyond imagination. They have no concept that it represents fullness, richness, pleasures, and over-flowing with plenty, both physically and spiritually. They have no idea that boundless energy is available to them if they will but tap it.

Here is what Paul wrote to Timothy in this regard: *"For God has not given us the spirit of fear; but of power, and of love, and of a sound mind"* (*2 Timothy 1:7*). This verse is not about how to tap the better "inner you." It is not about practicing "pull yourself up by your boot-straps" positive thinking derived from human strength. In the long run, these are not worth much. On their own people fall short, and ultimately fail in the most important aspects of life. They are powerless to overcome weaknesses and faults—and to triumph in the end. Paul is speaking about drawing upon God's Spirit within a converted mind, and using it as a source of strength—of real power! He wrote the Ephesians to *"be strong in the Lord, and in the power of His might"* (*Ephesians 6:10*). This can be you. Enormous inner strength and power will flow into and through you, if you take advantage of the access that God offers.

Read what Christ told His disciples about how God's Spirit worked within them: *"He that believes on Me, as the scripture has said, out of his belly shall flow rivers of living water. (But this spoke He of the Spirit, which they that believe on Him should receive ...)"* (*John 7:38-39*). Have you ever stood by a powerful river and watched the current? I have many times. A big river carries enormous power and force, and Christ under-stood this when He chose this analogy. God's Spirit flows like a river, and it produces mightily in the lives of those who have it. It radiates out of one who has it and brings love, faith, joy, and peace from its Source, God. This Spirit will help you meet challenges, defeat enemies, conquer fear, and reflect cheerfulness. It will bring wisdom, knowledge, and un-derstanding, and drive anger, bitterness, and anxiety away. It will replace discouragement with energy and hope. It will bring zeal to accomplish and remove confusion and indifference. It will take shattered dreams and shriveled feelings, and expand them to new horizons—and bring an ex-pectation of success. It will take stress and turn it into productivity and fulfilling accomplishment.

In *James 1:17*, God says that He gives every good and perfect gift. Peo-ple cannot offer or bring to you the truly good things of life, but God can. He says that He will if you come to Him and ask for help when you are in "time of need." His answers are satisfying, and His strength is real, life

-changing. How sad that the lives of so many are so completely empty; so utterly devoid of joy, happiness, and abundance. Many try drugs, fall into immoral lifestyles, pursue the wrong kind of entertainment, commit crimes, and otherwise get into trouble, simply because they are bored. They have no idea that their lives can be filled with purpose. This lack of understanding is so unnecessary, so far from what God intended for every human being. Notice what Isaiah wrote: *"... everyone that thirsts, come you to the waters, and he that has no money; come you, buy, and eat; yes, come, buy wine and milk without money and without price"* (*Isaiah 55:1*). You too can come to God and "buy" His "waters" (His Holy Spirit) when you have "no money." Isaiah continues by asking, *"Wherefore do you spend money for that which is not bread? And your labor for that which satisfies not?"* (*Isaiah 55:2*). Billions do this continually.

This has been a critical principle that I have had to learn. I lead a very active, busy life. I am generally able to work long hours, day after day, for long periods. But this was not possible (and would never be possible) until I learned to claim God's promise and tap His strength for the physical energy needed on a daily basis. Take a moment to read *Isaiah 40:28-31*, and then claim God's promise to renew the *"weary,"* the *"faint,"* and those with *"no might,"* if they come to Him.

A Wonderful Way of Life

The vitality, abundance, and pure joyful happiness that can be yours is closer than you think. But you must recognize that God offers an entirely new and different way of life. It means living *"by every word that proceeds out of the mouth of God"* (*Matthew 4:4; Luke 4:4; Deuteronomy 8:3*). This means studying God's Word and drinking in its meaning. It means praying daily and seeking God with your whole heart and resisting Satan the devil.

This also means periodically accepting the Bible's correction, which can sometimes cut very deep (*Hebrews 4:12*). But the converted mind seeks to grow at every opportunity, and receiving correction is also directly connected to happiness. Notice: *"Behold, happy is the man whom God corrects: therefore despise not you the chastening of the Almighty"* (*Job 5:17*). Of course, no one naturally enjoys correction, but yielding to it produces a by-product described as the *"peaceable fruit of righteousness"* (*Hebrews 12:9-11*). So, if even correction can bring happiness, just think of the joy that will come from practicing the many other aspects of the Christian way of life.

Practicing God's Way will lead you to be concerned for those around you. You will move away from self-interest and replace it with an interest in others. You will want to humble yourself and value the lives of others, more than your own opinions, and your own needs. You will feel good will and cheerfulness in your heart. You will want to smile, lead a life of vigor, and reflect calm when standing in the eye of a storm. You will find courage to step out in full and complete faith, knowing that God is with you and you are not alone. It means understanding that you *"can do all things through Christ who strengthens [you]"* (*Philippians 4:13*) and that *"with God all things are possible"* (*Matthew 19:26*). Those around you cannot help but see these things. You will become an example to them, a light (*Matthew 5:14*) in a world so obviously growing darker every day (*John 3:19-21; 9:4*). They will see that you have found meaning and purpose in a confused, disagreeing, unhappy world! And knowing that you are doing this will bring its own happiness and satisfaction to you, because it is what God intends for His servants. Confidence will flow from this, but not self-confidence.

You will not find yourself constantly carping, griping, moaning, and complaining about life's endless "injustices." You will not want to speak evil of others, but will want to lift them up, rather than pull or put them down. You will be able to conquer loneliness. And this conduct will generate a never-before-realized strength, boldness, and confidence that will literally drive your life. This may cause people to ask you for help, encouragement, or advice. They may see that your life is "together," while theirs is not. People are drawn to strength, they are drawn to confidence. If you exude these things, radiating a power that is greater than anything they have seen, they may seek your help. They will ask for your help, and they may even ask why you are filled with hope and cheerfulness (*1 Peter 3:15*).

Be sure that you do not go around pushing your beliefs and values on others. This will turn them off, and drive them away, producing the opposite of what you are trying to achieve. But if people see that you always give others the benefit of the doubt, and are always willing to offer a helping hand, they will recognize you as being different than everyone else. While they may not appreciate your doctrinal beliefs, they will very much appreciate your radiant attitude.

Remembering the Supreme Goal

Finally, you will always remember why God put you on Earth, why He gave you life. You will want to seek salvation, with zeal, vigor, enthusiasm, and drive, led by hope and faith, as though final success depends on your conduct every day. You will not want to compromise God's Way or His truth; and you will enjoy richness and fullness overflowing as a result of this determined approach. This will give you more strength to address your problems and overcome them.

Paul wrote to the Thessalonians to *"rejoice evermore" (1 Thessalonians 5:16)*. This is one of the only two verses in the Bible that contains two words, making it hard to forget. Yet it is a command from God to all those begotten of His Spirit. It is why a thousand years earlier, the Psalmist approached each day by saying, *"This is the day which the Lord has made; we will rejoice and be glad in it" (Psalms 118:24)*. In the very next verse, he asked God to *"send now prosperity"*. These are not vague, nebulous scriptures. They are clear, direct, and plain, and vital instruction for you and me. John added, *"truly our fellowship is with the Father, and with His Son Jesus Christ.... that your joy may be full" (1 John 1:3-4)*. Your joy can be full, beyond your wildest dreams, if you walk and fellowship with God and Christ as a constant way of life that overarches your every word and deed.

Yes, you can live the rich, radiant, full, happy, joyful, abundant life. All you must do is be willing to leave the old way of life behind. Go to the source and begin!

www.ingramcontent.com/pod-product-compliance
Lightning Source LLC
Chambersburg PA
CBHW061747020426
42331CB00006B/1390